BEHIND THE INVASION OF IRAQ

BEHIND THE INVASION OF IRAQ

RESEARCH UNIT FOR POLITICAL ECONOMY

Monthly Review Press
New York

© Copyright 2003 by Research Unit for Political Economy
All Rights Reserved
Library of Congress Cataloging-in-Publication data
available from the publisher
ISBN 1-58367-093-9 (pbk)

Monthly Review Press
122 West 27th Street
New York, NY 10001
Production & Design Terry J. Allen

www.monthlyreview.org
Printed in Canada
10 9 8 7 6 5 4 3 2

TABLE OF CONTENTS

About the Research Unit for Political Economy

The Research Unit for Political Economy (RUPE) was set up in Mumbai (Bombay), India, in the late 1980s, with the aim of explaining the economy in simple terms that could be grasped by ordinary working people, connecting problems as they are directly encountered by people with the underlying political economy that is responsible for them. RUPE's main target audience is the activists of various people's struggles, who want to spell out the connections between their particular struggles and the larger processes of which those struggles are a part.

RUPE is run on the voluntary labor of a handful of people, and on a shoestring budget collected from a large number of individual contributions. Those of us who work for RUPE are also active in the working class movement, the democratic rights movement, and various movements in solidarity with people's struggles.

PREFACE

Over the past three decades, the handful of Monthly Review Press books and copies of *Monthly Review* which found their way to India would pass from hand to hand, be read and re-read, photocopied and circulated, till they were dog-eared from use. For MR Press books were for use: use by those struggling to change the existing world order ruled by imperialism—a term *Monthly Review* not only employed but did much to substantiate.

We were therefore happy when MR Press offered to bring out this brief publication, for it, too, was written very much for *use*. We had an immediate object in mind. Just as there is an unprecedented worldwide upsurge today against the impending assault on Iraq, there is available a remarkable wealth of material on various aspects of that assault and on the current global drive of the United States: exposés of the U.S. government's strategic designs; investigations of the U.S. plans to use weapons of mass destruction (precisely the crime it accuses its opponents of); refutations of each of the U.S. propaganda offensives; and meticulous documentation of the terrible price paid by the targeted peoples. Carried out by a multitude of organizations and individuals, this activity is in a sense a vast collaborative effort, even in the absence of any central coordination.

In this book we have attempted to summarize the most important elements from this wealth of material. But more importantly, we have attempted to integrate all these elements into a consistent interpretation of what is taking place.

To many, the current U.S. offensive may seem "mad," and indeed it is so from the standpoint of humanity. However, it is hardly the work of one man or of a tiny clique. The U.S. Congress, no less, in effect voted to hand over to Bush its own power to declare war. That sort of bipartisan surrender does not happen without forces working behind the scenes. One must search for the causes of the war not in some individual or collective madness but in the interests of giant American corporations that essentially define the character of the U.S. economy, and in the current situation of the U.S. economy as part of the world economy. That is what we have attempted to do here.

Once we understand clearly what we are struggling against, and where it comes from, we are better placed to know how to struggle. Can more thorough weapons inspections in Iraq satisfy the United States and head off a war? No, since eliminating weapons of mass destruction has nothing to do with the United States' real objectives in West Asia. Will the United States be easily dissuaded from invading and occupying Iraq and other countries in West Asia? No, because there are profound economic reasons for the United States' current plans. Why are the governments of France, Germany, Russia and China lined up against the American position? Not because they possess a conscience, but because they grasp how their interests are threatened by the hidden agenda of the U.S. superpower's current drive.

Finally, understanding the political economy of this war would help one understand the underlying basis of future wars, and much else about how the world is ruled today. Many who have come out to oppose the invasion of Iraq are through their experience slowly awakening to the fact that the roots of such unjust wars lie in the world order itself, what we would call the imperialist system. To achieve its aims, that system employs at times "peaceful" means, at times war; indeed the exemplary effect of war bolsters the effectiveness of "peaceful" means. Any regime in Latin America which contemplates disregarding the instructions of the International Monetary Fund must be prepared for some form of war—internal subversion, proxy war, or even direct invasion by the United States. *Imperialist war, then, is the military arm of what is being termed "globalization."* In fact, just as imperialist globalization demands absolute freedom for capital to flow in and out of countries without barriers placed by people's economic interests and rights, impe-rialist states are now demanding the freedom for their troops to move in and out of countries without interference by national sovereignties. And while the privatization program dictated by the IMF in various Third World countries cannot be equated with the U.S. plans for the invasion of Iraq, the two are similar in one respect: the appropriation of the country's assets by imperialism.

We hope, then, that this book will help some of those coming forward in the burgeoning anti-war movement today to look further than this war, and at the system that gives rise to it.

*

This book first appeared as a special issue of the journal *Aspects of India's Economy*, which is brought out by the Research Unit for Political Economy, Mumbai, India. Why a journal on the Indian economy should bring out a special issue on the impending invasion of Iraq requires some explanation, which we provided in our original preface. Even as the United States pre-pares to launch a massive assault on Iraq, it has declared India to be its most important ally in this region. This despite the fact that the United States has three bases in Pakistan at the moment. Asia is of increasing importance in the United States' global priorities, and India has become an important part of the U.S. plans for Asia. In particular, the United States intends to recruit India in its encirclement and checking of China, as it anticipates that China would develop into a threat to U.S. hegemony in this region.

The Indian rulers, for their part, are eager to be anointed U.S. satraps in the region, and are playing along. On matters of economic policy, of course, Indian governments of all hues have been under IMF-World Bank tutelage for a long time now, more blatantly so since the 1991 structural adjustment loan from the Fund. (A striking instance of more direct American tutelage was the notorious deal with Enron for the setting up of a power plant in western India. That deal, guaranteeing extortionate prof-its to Enron and bankruptcy for the state government, was pushed through not only with bribes to a number of Indian political parties but with direct and repeated intervention by U.S. officials.)

In recent years military and political ties, too, between India and the United States have grown apace. A number of joint exercises between the two militaries are taking place; the two navies have been jointly patrolling the Malacca Straits; American warships now routinely refuel in Chennai (Madras) and Mumbai (Bombay); the United States has cleared the sale to India of high technology with military applications; the two countries' defense intelligence agencies share information; U.S. army personnel are to be allowed to train in a base in the north-east of India near the border with China; and a joint working group "to combat terrorism" has been at work since February 2000. Hand in hand with this, India's military ties with Israel have blossomed, and the latter is now India's second biggest source of weapons imports.

India's rulers used the events of September 11, 2001 to identify themselves even more closely with the U.S. cause. India's Cabinet Committee on Security Affairs met two days after on September 13, and unconditionally offered "all cooperation and facilities for any U.S. military operation," without any such request from the United States. For the Indian rulers, who have little else to offer the Indian people, their hold on power has been based on whipping up hatred of Muslims and Pakistan. Support for the U.S invasion of Afghanistan dovetailed neatly with their domestic political platform. The Vishwa Hindu Parishad (VHP), a fanatical body linked to the ruling party in India, refers the United States' George Bush, Israel's Ariel Sharon and Russia's Vladimir Putin as its three heroes—for what they did to Muslims in Afghanistan, the West Bank/Gaza, and Chechnya. The VHP emulated its heroes in March 2002: It carried out a pogrom of an estimated 2,000 Muslims in the western Indian state of Gujarat. Significantly, the Indian prime minister not only blamed the Muslims themselves for provoking these killings, but linked them to international developments: "Wherever there are Muslims, there is a problem . . . the kind of Islam being perpetrated in the world today is a violent, intolerant Islam that has no room for tolerance."

Indeed, so thoroughly did the Indian state identify itself with the U.S. bombing and invasion of Afghanistan in 2001 that it arrested leftist students in Delhi for distributing leaflets against the war, disrupted a protest against the war by Muslims in the textile town Malegaon in Maharashtra (this provoked riots, followed by police firing on Muslims), banned the Students' Islamic Movement of India on a flimsy pretext, banned two Marxist-Leninist organisations, revived a much-reviled repressive law in the name of controlling terrorism, and intensified repression in Kashmir. It thus showed how it could integrate its interests with the declared crusade of the U.S. government.

Indo-U.S. "cooperation" now extends to India's internal security. The U.S. Federal Bureau of Investigation (FBI) has set up office in Delhi, the purpose of which is as yet a mystery. Israel's security agencies are closely involved in India-controlled Kashmir, where the Indian government has been trying to suppress an insurgency. In the coming days, this integration of Indian internal security with U.S. agencies is set to increase.

Most significant of all is the Indian government's decision to endorse the U.S. missile defense program. In turn, the United States has dropped all objections to India's nuclear weapons program, and indeed the U.S. ambassador promotes India as the U.S. partner "to curtail the proliferation of Weapons of Mass Destruction in Asia, and the means to deliver them." Evidently India is being promised protection by the U.S. missile shield.

It is not difficult to understand the principal target of the U.S.-India alliance. "Vajpayee's nuclear strategy is centered wholly on China," writes the *Washington Post* (September 7, 2001). Indeed, in the wake of India's May 11, 1998, nuclear tests, the Indian prime minister wrote an abject secret letter to the then U.S. president Clinton, explaining that the real target of the Indian nuclear program was China. The *Post* notes that "China sees the Bush strategic defense plan as aimed specifically at neutralizing its small but growing nuclear arsenal. A significant warming of U.S.-Indian ties, powered by conceptual agreement on missile defense, could cause the Chinese to expand and accelerate their nuclear upgrades, to poke at India through help to Pakistan and take risks that have not been well calculated."

In the face of a U.S. offensive, a U.S.-India axis, and a missile shield, China might follow a course similar to that followed by the USSR in the

1980s—namely, building up a much larger force of nuclear missiles in order to penetrate the missile shield in different places, including over India. The American government is well aware that such a program would be enormously expensive, and would strain China's resources; indeed, that is one of its objectives. The Indian people, however, are unaware that they are being thrust into this dangerous strategic chess-game by their rulers.

Against this background, the current U.S. strategic agenda globally has direct implications for the Indian people, and they need to study its implications.

*

It almost seems inappropriate for us to acknowledge the contribution of Jacob Levich, a New York-based writer, editor, and activist, to preparation of this text. He worked virtually as a member of our team, e-mailing us some *1,500* carefully selected articles on topics relevant to this issue, hunting down instantly any information we requested, and sharing his own valuable insights freely. He is not responsible, of course, for any errors in what we have written.

Rajani X. Desai,
Editor, *Aspects of India's Economy.*
February 15, 2003—the day of unprecedented worldwide protest against U.S. imperialism.

1. Introduction

U.S. imperialism has announced its intention to launch an invasion of Iraq and to change the regime there. The impending invasion is the culmination of U.S. efforts for the last decade.

The 1991 U.S. attack on Iraq in the name of evacuating Kuwait not only caused a terrible immediate loss of life but systematically and deliberately devastated the entire civilian infrastructure of Iraq. Eleven years of sanctions have already wreaked unparalleled devastation in the country's economic life and effected what a senior UN official termed "genocide" by systematically starving the country of elementary needs. Iraq is not free to spend the earnings from sale of its own oil in the way it wishes. "No-fly zones" and repeated bombings devoid of all legal cover have violated the country's sovereignty and security. Under U.S.-U.K. protection, pro-U.S. Kurdish forces hold sway in northern Iraq. In the guise of "weapons inspection," brazen espionage has been carried out by the United States, U.K., and Israel.

Now, however, we are about to witness a major new development, with far-reaching consequences: the direct imperialist occupation of the whole of Iraq. Further, it is widely reported in the American press that the United States plans to use the invasion of Iraq as a launching pad for a drastic reshaping of West Asia. The Bush administration is actively considering invading various countries and replacing regimes in the entire region—Iran, Saudi Arabia, Syria, Libya, Egypt, and Lebanon are among the countries to be targeted. This is to be accompanied by Israel carrying out some form of "final solution" to the Palestinian question—whether in the form of mass eviction or colonization.

The justifications U.S. imperialism is advancing for the impending assault on Iraq are absurd, often contradictory. Unlike in the case of the 1991 Gulf War or the 2001 bombing and invasion of Afghanistan, this time the United States lacks even the fig leaf of an excuse for its aggression. The major American and British media corporations have once again come forward as foot soldiers in the campaign.

Apart from the U.K. and Israel, countries in the rest of the world have either opposed the planned assault or at least attempted to distance themselves from it; public opinion outside the United States and Israel is set against the war, and even within the highly indoctrinated United States opinion is rapidly shifting; indeed the world, including the United States, has seen a remarkable wave of protest before the start of the war. Most significantly, there are signs that a long-delayed popular upsurge is imminent in West Asia. While various Arab client states have under U.S. pressure now muted their opposition, and some will offer facilities for the assault, they evidently fear the wrath of their own people. It is clear that for the U.S. rulers the entire operation will entail not only huge expenditures but grave political risks. Yet they are determined to press on.

Although some voices of caution were sounded at first among senior strategic experts and political figures in the United States, there now appears to be broad consensus among the U.S. ruling classes regarding this extraordinary adventurism and unilateral aggression. The manner in which the U.S. president was able to ram through Congress his demand for sweeping and open-ended war powers makes clear that the corporate sector as a whole (not only the oil companies) is vitally interested in the war. It is significant that despite recession and economic uncertainty, despite deepening budget and balance of payments deficits, the United States is willing to foot the bill for a massive, open-ended military operation. Evidently U.S. corporations believe the potential reward will justify the war; or that the failure to go to war will have grave consequences for them.

It is more or less publicly acknowledged that the immediate reward is a massive oil grab, of a scale not witnessed since the days of colonialism. Caspian prospects pale in comparison with Iraqi oil wealth. Iraq has the world's second largest reserves (at present 115 billion barrels, but long-delayed exploration may take that figure to 220-250 billion barrels). Moreover, its oil is, along with that of Saudi Arabia, Kuwait, and Iran, by far the cheapest to extract. The United States is quite openly offering the French and Russians, who have giant contracts with the present regime that cannot be realized under sanctions, slices of the post-invasion cake in exchange for their approval in the Security Council.

Control of petroleum resources and pipeline routes is obviously a central consideration in U.S. imperialist designs worldwide—note the long-term installation of U.S. forces from Afghanistan through Central Asia to the Balkans; the entry of U.S. troops in the Philippines and the pressure on Indonesia to involve the United States in a campaign against Islamic fundamentalists in the region; the drive for U.S. military intervention in Colombia and the attempt to oust Chavez in Venezuela. (The systematic drive by the United States in northern Latin America has close parallels with its campaign in West Asia.) The United States is particularly anxious to install a large contingent of troops near Saudi Arabia, anticipating the collapse of, or drastic change in, the regime there. Saudi Arabia has the world's greatest stock of oil wealth. Indeed the United States is contemplating using the invasion of Iraq as the springboard for a drastic political "cleansing" of the entire region, along the lines of the process long under way in the Balkans and continuing in Afghanistan-Pakistan. Indeed, it is even willing to provoke, by its invasion of Iraq, uprisings in other states of the region in order to provide it with an occasion to invade those states. All this is not speculation, but has been explicitly spelled out in various policy documents authored by or commissioned by those now in charge of the U.S. military and foreign policy.

Linked to the above is a further, strategic, dimension to the U.S. aggressive designs. Not only is the United States increasingly dependent on West Asian oil for its own consumption; its capture of West Asian oil is also intended to secure its supremacy among imperialist powers.

The global crisis of overproduction is showing up the underlying weakness of the United States real economy, as a result of which U.S. trade and budget deficits are galloping. The euro now poses a credible alternative to the status of the dollar as the global reserve currency, threatening the United States' crucial ability to fund its deficits by soaking up the world's savings. The United States anticipates that the capture of Iraq, and whatever else it has in store for the region, will directly benefit its corporations (oil, arms, engineering, financial) even as it shuts out the corporations from other imperialist countries. Further, it intends to prevent the bulk of petroleum trade from being conducted in euros and thus maintain the dollar's supremacy. In a broader sense, it believes that such a reassertion of its supremacy (in military terms and in control of strategic resources) will prevent the emergence of any serious imperialist challenger such as the EU. In that sense the present campaign is in line with the Pentagon's 1992 Defense Planning Guidance, which called for preventing any other major power from acquiring the strength to develop into a challenger to the United States's solitary supremacy. (A European foothold even in Iran could bring about a euro-based oil economy; this perhaps explains the puzzling inclusion of Iran in the "axis of evil.")

For these very reasons, the United States is facing more serious opposition from France, Germany, and Russia in relation to Iraq than on any strategic issue in the past. Since the collapse of the Soviet Union no imperialist power has had the military muscle to oppose U.S. unilateralism, and other powers have focused instead on getting their minor share of the spoils of the former Soviet empire and the intensified plunder of the third world. However, these powers see that the present campaign is intended precisely to shut them out of contention for equal status with the United States in the long term as well. Contention for such status is the very reason for the EU's existence.

At the same time direct control over the region's petroleum resources will give the United States another important lever to use against China, which will become considerably more dependent on petroleum imports during the next decade. The United States also sees capitalist China as a potential threat to its plans for domination of East and Southeast Asia. The United States has taken various steps to block China's plans to obtain independent (i.e., not controlled by the United States), stable access to West Asian oil or Caspian oil. The United States has already installed its military throughout oil- and gas-rich Central Asia; now it is in the process of doing so in vastly richer West Asia.

Although certain circumstances have led the United States to navigate a resolution on Iraq through the UN Security Council, the United States has now openly declared the death of the UN system, for what it was worth: this was the content of Bush's speech to the UN, where he declared that it would be irrelevant unless it rubber-stamped U.S. supremacy. The new doctrine is contained in the U.S. National Security Strategy document, which declares the right of American pre-emptive strikes against "emerging" or potential threats, and warns that it is willing to act unilaterally if other imperialist powers do not follow its lead. In line with the new doctrine, the United States is systematically revising the existing international consensus on use of nuclear weapons.

In order to carry out its plan, the United States, already over extended, will have to extend itself even further. Not only has it rapidly multiplied its military outposts and involvements across the world, from the Philippines to Asia (Central, South, and West) to Latin America, but it has taken on the status of a direct occupier in Afghanistan, and evidently intends to do so in at least Iraq. Thus it both spreads its forces thin and calls forth much fiercer nationalist resistance than under the indirect rule common in the neo colonial order. Anticipating the heavy costs of their new mission, intellectual hacks of the U.S. and U.K. ruling classes are busy preparing theoretical justifications for a new bout of colonialism. At the same time the internal repressive apparatus is being strengthened in the United States and panic, submission to authority, and other elements of fascism are being manufactured.

The simultaneous emergence of worldwide popular opposition and resistance, opposition from other imperialist powers, and profound weakness in the U.S. economy suggest that events will not develop as U.S. imperialism wishes.

2. WESTERN IMPERIALISM AND IRAQ

Three themes stand out in Iraq's history over the last century, in the light of the present U.S. plans to invade and occupy that country.

First, the attempt by imperialist powers to dominate Iraq in order to grab its vast oil wealth. As regards this there is hardly a dividing line between oil corporations and their home governments, with the governments undertaking to promote, secure, and militarily protect their oil corporations.

Second, the attempt by each imperialist power to exclude others from the prize.

Third, the vibrancy of nationalist opposition among the people of Iraq and indeed the entire region to these designs of imperialism. This is manifested at times in mass upsurges and at other times in popular pressure on whomever is in power to demand better terms from the oil companies or even to expropriate them.

The following account is limited to Iraq, and it provides only the barest sketch.

FROM COLONY TO SEMI-COLONY

Entry of Imperialism

Iraq, the easternmost country of the Arab world, was home to perhaps the world's first great civilization. It was known in classical times as Mesopotamia ("Land between the Rivers"—the Tigris and the Euphrates), and became known as Iraq in the seventh century. For centuries Baghdad was a rich and vibrant city, the intellectual center of the Arab world. From the sixteenth century to 1918, Iraq was a part of the Turkish Ottoman Empire, divided into three *vilayets* (provinces): Mosul in the north, Baghdad in the center, and Basra in the south. The first was predominantly Kurdish, the second predominantly Sunni Arab, and the third predominantly Shiite Arab.

As the Ottoman Empire fell into decline, Britain and France began extending their influence into its territories, constructing massive projects such as railroads and the Suez Canal and keeping the Arab countries deep in debt to British and French banks.

At the beginning of the twentieth century Britain directly ruled Egypt, Sudan, and the Persian Gulf, while France was the dominant power in Lebanon and Syria. Iran was divided between British and Russian spheres of influence. The carving up of the Ottoman territories (from Turkey to the Arabian peninsula) was on the agenda of the imperialist powers.

When Germany, a relative latecomer to the imperialist dining table, attempted to extend its influence in the region by obtaining a "concession" to build a railway from Europe to Baghdad, Britain was alarmed.[1] By this time the British government—in particular its navy—had realized the strategic importance of oil, and it was thought that the region might be rich in oil. Britain invested, 2.2 million in the Anglo-Persian Oil Company (a fully British firm operating in Iran) to obtain a 51 percent stake in the company. Gulbenkian, an adventurous Armenian entrepreneur, argued that there must be oil in Iraq as well. At his initiative the Turkish Petroleum Company (TPC) was formed: 50 percent British, 25 percent German, and 25 percent Royal Dutch-Shell (Dutch- and British-owned).

World War I (1914-1918) underlined for the imperialists the importance of control of oil for military purposes, and hence the urgency of controlling the sources of oil. As soon as war was declared with the Ottomans, Britain landed a force (composed largely of Indian soldiers) in southern Iraq, and eventually took Baghdad in 1917. It took Mosul in November 1918, in violation of the armistice with the Turks a week earlier.

During the war the British carried on two contradictory sets of secret negotiations. The first was with Sharif Husayn of Mecca. In exchange for Arab revolt against Turkey, the British promised support for Arab independence after the war. However, the British insisted that Baghdad and Basra would be special zones of British interest where "special administrative arrangements" would be necessary to "safeguard our mutual economic interests."

The second set of secret negotiations, in flagrant violation of the above, was between the British and the French. In the Sykes–Picot Agreement of 1916, Iraq was carved up between the two powers, with the Mosul *vilayet* going to France and the other two to Britain. For its assent czarist Russia was to be compensated with territory in northeast Turkey. When the Bolshevik revolutionaries seized power in November 1917 and published the czarist regime's secret treaties, including the Sykes–Picot Agreement, the Arabs learned how they had been betrayed.

Iraq Under British Rule

After the war, the spoils of the German and Ottoman empires were divided among the victors. Britain's promises during the war that Arabs would get independence were swiftly buried. France got the mandate for Syria and Lebanon, and Britain got the mandate for Palestine and Iraq. (The "mandate" system, a thin disguise for colonial rule, was created under the League of Nations, the predecessor to today's United Nations. Mandate territories, earlier the possessions of the Ottomans were to be "guided" by the victorious imperialist powers till they had proved themselves capable of self-rule.)

Britain threatened to go to war to ensure that Mosul province, which was known to contain oil, remained in Iraq. The French conceded Mosul in exchange for British support of French dominance in Lebanon and Syria and a 25 percent French share in TPC.

However, anti-imperialist agitation in Iraq troubled the British from the start. In 1920, with the announcement that Britain had been awarded the mandate for Iraq, revolt broke out against the British rulers and became widespread. The British suppressed the rebellion ruthlessly—

among other things bombing Iraqi villages from the air (as they had done a year earlier to suppress the Rowlatt agitation in the Punjab). In 1920, Secretary of State for War and Air Winston Churchill proposed that Mesopotamia "could be cheaply policed by aircraft armed with gas bombs, supported by as few as 4,000 British and 10,000 Indian troops," a policy formally adopted at the 1921 Cairo conference.[2]

The British Install a Ruler

Shaken by the revolt, the British felt it wise to put up a facade. (In the words of Curzon, the foreign secretary, Britain wanted in the Arab territories an "Arab facade ruled and administered under British guidance and controlled by a native Mohammedan and, as far as possible, by an Arab staff.... There should be no actual incorporation of the conquered territory in the dominions of the conqueror, but the absorption may be veiled by such constitutional fictions as a protectorate, a sphere of influence, a buffer state and so on.") The British High Commissioner proclaimed Emir Faisal I, belonging to the Hashemite family of Mecca, which had been expelled from the French mandate Syria, as the King of Iraq. The puppet Faisal promptly signed a treaty of alliance with Britain that largely reproduced the terms of the mandate. This roused such strong nationalist protests that the cabinet was forced to resign, and the British High Commissioner assumed dictatorial powers for several years. Nationalist leaders were deported from the country on a wide scale. (In this period the whole region was in ferment, with anti-imperialist struggles emerging in Palestine and Syria as well.) The British also drafted a constitution for Iraq that gave the King quasi-dictatorial powers over the Parliament.

In 1925, widespread demonstrations in Baghdad for complete independence delayed the treaty's approval by the Constituent Assembly. The High Commissioner could only force ratification by threatening to dissolve the assembly. Even before the treaty of alliance was ratified—and before there was even the facade of an Iraqi government—a new concession was granted to the Turkish Petroleum Company for the whole of Iraq, in the face of widespread opposition and the resignation of two members of the cabinet. (Among other things, the British blackmailed Iraq by threatening that they would, in the negotiations with the Turks, cede the oil-rich northern province of Mosul to neighboring Turkey—the opposite of what they were demanding in the earlier-mentioned negotiations with the French. Thus even the borders of the countries in these regions were set at the convenience of imperialist exploitation. The worst sufferers were the Kurds, whose territory was divided by the imperialist powers among southern Turkey, northern Syria, northern Iraq, and northwestern Iran.)

The terms of the concession, covering virtually the entire country till the year 2000, were outrageous. Payment was four shillings (one-fifth of a British pound) per ton of oil produced. For this extraordinary giveaway, the puppet king Faisal received a personal present of £40,000. It was this concession the oil corporations for half a century thereafter would fight to defend as their "legitimate" right.

Contention for Oil

With Germany's defeat in the war its stake in the Turkish Petroleum Company fell into Britain's lap. Thus Britain would almost completely dominate the company. However, this was no longer tenable following the new correlation of the strengths of the different imperialist powers. Britain, though it had the largest empire among the imperialist powers, was actually in decline. Unable now to compete with other industrial economies, it desperately attempted to use its exclusive grip over its colonies to shore up its economic strength; whereas the United States, now the leading capitalist power, demanded what it termed an "open door" to exploit the possessions of the older colonizing powers.[3] Two years after the end of World War I Woodrow Wilson, the American president, wrote:

> It is evident to me that we are on the eve of a commercial war of the severest sort and I am afraid that Great Britain will prove capable of as great commercial savagery as Germany has displayed for so many years in her commercial methods.[4]

American oil companies, with U.S. government backing, demanded a share in the Turkish Petroleum Company, and by 1928 two American companies, Jersey Standard and Socony (later known as Exxon and Mobil, and today as the merged Exxon-Mobil) got a 23.75 percent stake, on par with the British, French, and Royal Dutch-Shell interests. Most of the major oil corporations in the world were thus represented in the Turkish Petroleum Company (now renamed the Iraq Petroleum Company—hereafter IPC).

Contending with Nationalism

The continuous local opposition to British rule at last forced Britain to grant Iraq "independence" in 1932. But this Britain did only after extracting a new treaty stipulating a "close alliance" between the two countries and a "common defense position"—effectively, continued indirect rule by the British. Britain kept its bases at Basra and west of the Euphrates, and Faisal continued to occupy the Iraqi throne.

After the war ended in 1945, British occupation continued. Martial law was declared to crush protests against the developments in Palestine in 1948 (the driving out of the Palestinians and the seizure of their lands by the new Zionist state). Just then, the Iraqi government signed a new treaty of alliance with Britain, whereby Iraq was not to take any step in foreign policy contrary to British directions. A joint British-Iraqi defense board was to be set up. But when the prime minister returned from London after having concluded this deal, a popular uprising took place in Baghdad, forcing his resignation and the repudiation of the treaty. In the following years, nationalist forces demanded nationalization of the oil industry (as Iran had carried out in 1951).

In 1952 occurred another popular uprising, carried out by students and "extremists." The police were unable to control the demonstrators, and the regent called on the army to maintain public order. The chief of the armed forces general staff governed the country under martial law for more than two months. All political parties were suppressed in 1954.

Growing U.S. Intervention in the Region

The price of standing up to the oil corporations was made clear in neighboring Iran. There the regime headed by Mossadeq nationalized British

Petroleum in 1951, faced a devastating boycott by all the oil giants for the next two years, and was overthrown by a CIA-led coup in 1953. (The CIA man in charge of the operation later became vice-president of Gulf Oil.)[5]

On the other hand, regimes throughout the region were under pressure from the Arab masses. Gamal Abdul Nasser, who came to power in Egypt in a 1952 coup, adopted a confrontational posture toward the United States and Britain, nationalizing the Suez Canal and taking assistance from the Soviet Union. Nasser's stance won him popular support in the Arab world, where Iraq and Egypt contended for leadership. In that period an anti-imperialist wave swept the Arab countries, threatening the stability of pro-Western puppet regimes.

The United States became the new gendarme of the region to suppress any agitation against imperialism and its client states. For example, when in 1953 both Saudi Arabia and Iraq crushed oil workers' strikes by the use of troops and martial law regimes, shipments of arms from the United States to both followed immediately. In 1957 the Jordanian king (the first cousin of the Iraqi king) arrested his prime minister, dissolved the parliament, outlawed political parties, and threw his opponents into concentration camps, with economic and military aid from the United States. In 1958 the right-wing Lebanese regime used American equipment in its attempt to crush nationalist opposition. At American insistence three pro-U.S./UK regimes—Iraq, Turkey, and Pakistan—came together to form an alliance against the USSR, the Baghdad Pact (later known as the Mideast Treaty Organization and the Central Treaty Organization; Britain and Iran were later to join). Iraq, the only Arab country to join this pact, had to face Nasser s denunciation for doing so.

TOWARD NATIONALIZATION

In July 1958 an army faction led by Abdel Karim Qasim seized power in Iraq, executed the king and Nuri as-Said, and declared a republic to wide public acclaim. This was the first overthrow of a puppet regime in an oil-producing country. The new regime appealed to the popular anti-imperialist consciousness in its very first announcement: "With the aid of God Almighty and the support of the people and the armed services, we have liberated the country from the domination of a corrupt group which was installed by imperialism to lull the people."

The United States and the U.K. immediately moved their troops to Lebanon and Jordan respectively in preparation to invade Iraq. Unfortunately for the United States, the deposed regime was so widely despised in Iraq that no force could be found to assist the American plan. Nevertheless, the United States delivered an ultimatum threatening intervention if the new regime did not respect its oil interests. The coup leaders for their part issued repeated declarations that these interests would in fact not be touched. Only then were American and British troops withdrawn. Thus Iraq is no stranger to the threat of imperialist invasion.

Popular Pressure and the Companies' Counter Attack

Despite its assurances to the Americans, the new Iraqi regime remained under popular pressure. The Iraqi masses expected the downfall of the puppet king to result in a renegotiation or scrapping of the colonial-era oil concession to the IPC. (According to Michael Tanzer, the total investment made by the oil companies in Iraq was less than $50 million—after this they received profits sufficient to finance all future investment;[6] whereas Joe Stork calculates their profits from Iraq at $322.9 million in 1963 alone.[7]) Even Iran and Saudi Arabia had obtained better terms than Iraq because their earlier concessions did not cover their entire territories, whereas IPC owned the entire territory of Iraq.

However, the owners of IPC, principally the American and British oil giants, owned fields elsewhere in the world as well, and it was not the cost of production but complex strategic considerations that determined which fields they would exploit first.[8] They were in no hurry to develop the Iraqi fields or build larger refining capacity there—IPC's existing installations covered only 0.5 percent of its concession area. When the Qasim regime demanded that the IPC give up 60 percent of its concession area, double output from existing installations and double refining capacity, the IPC responded by reducing output. The oil giants had decided to make an example of Iraq, to prevent any other oil-producing country from showing backbone.

Qasim responded to the oil giants' intransigence by withdrawing from the Baghdad Pact, withdrawing from the sterling bloc, signing an economic and technical aid deal with the Soviet Union in 1959, ordering British forces out of Habbaniya base, and canceling the American aid program. In 1961 he wound up negotiations with the IPC and issued Law 80, under which the IPC could continue to exploit its existing installations, but the remaining territory (99.5 percent) would revert to the government.[9]

The oil giants responded by further suppressing IPC production. In turn, Qasim in 1963 announced the formation of a new state oil company to develop the non-concession lands, and revealed an American note threatening Iraq with sanctions unless he changed his position. He was overthrown four days later in a coup that the Paris weekly *L'Express* stated flatly was "inspired by the CIA."[10]

1963 Coup and the IPC Negotiations

The coup was carried out by an alliance between the Ba'ath Party (full form: Arab Socialist Ba'ath Party; Ba'ath means "renaissance") and an army faction, but the Ba'ath was soon ejected from power by its partners in the coup. The new rulers promptly granted the IPC another 0.5 percent of the concession area, including the rich North Rumaila field which the IPC had discovered but failed to exploit. IPC agreed to enter a joint venture with the new Iraq National Oil Company (INOC) to explore and develop a large portion of the expropriated area as well.

The agreement, however, was condemned by Arab nationalist opinion, and the regime hesitated for years to ratify it. Meanwhile the Arab-Israeli War, in which Iraq participated, broke out in 1967. Israel, with American backing, seized and occupied lands belonging to Syria, Egypt, and Jordan. Diplomatic ties between Iraq and the United States were broken. The strength of anti-American and anti-British sentiment after the 1967 War made it impossible for the Iraqi regime to return North Rumaila to the IPC. The Iraqi government instead issued Law 97, whereby the INOC alone would develop oil in all but the 0.5 percent still conceded to the IPC.

Between 1961 and 1968, IPC increased production in Iraq by a fraction of the increase in production in the docile regimes of Iran, Kuwait, and

Saudi Arabia by the same oil giants who owned IPC. Since the size of IPC's payments to the Iraqi government depended on the size of its oil output, and since the government's revenues depended heavily on these payments, the oil giants' tactic caused Iraq great financial stringency, and prevented it from undertaking developmental projects. According to a secret U.S. government report, the IPC actually drilled wells to the wrong depth and covered others with bulldozers in order to reduce productive capacity. The prolonged deadlock had extracted a great price: "more than a dozen years of economic stagnation, political instability, and confrontation."[11]

Saddam Hussein Comes to Power

The Ba'ath party returned to power in a 1968 coup (in which Saddam Hussein became vice president, deputy head of the Revolutionary Command Council, and increasingly the real power), and that party continued the course toward extricating the oil industry from the grip of the IPC. Finally in 1972 the IPC was nationalized, its shareholders paid a compensation of $300 million (effectively offset by company payment of $345 million in back claims). The country turned to France and the Soviet Union for technical assistance and credit. The Soviets developed the North Rumaila field more or less on schedule by 1972.

For the Soviets, Iraq was an important breakthrough in the region: unlike Egypt and Syria, with whom the Soviets had ties (in the former they were ejected in 1972), Iraq had vast oil reserves. It thus yielded lucrative oil contracts, investments in Eastern Europe from its oil surpluses, massive arms sales, and the promise of greater Soviet influence in the region. France, too, maintained ties with Iraq's oil industry. (Significantly, despite the overwhelming importance of oil to Iraq's economy, and the heavy price of its dependence on foreign firms, the country did not bring about the level of technological self-reliance in this field that, during the same years, socialist China did. Rather, it merely attempted to loosen the bonds to the U.S./U.K. oil giants by tying up with other advanced countries.)

The Iraqi nationalization took place against the background of increasing assertion by even pro-U.S. regimes in the region. Radical Arab oil experts (most prominently Abdullah Tariki) gripped the popular imagination with their well-documented exposures of how the oil wealth of the Arab lands was being looted; the Organization of Petroleum Exporting Countries (OPEC) actively demanded better terms for their oil; a group of young army officers led by Muammar Qaddafi overthrew the Libyan monarchy in 1969 and called for confrontation with the oil giants; and the armed Palestinian struggle was born. The defeat of the Arab armies in the 1973 war with Israel further stoked anti-American sentiment. The process culminated with an Arab oil embargo against the Western states and a massive increase in prices paid to oil producing countries. Iraq, as a major oil producer (with the world's second-largest reserves, after Saudi Arabia), played a crucial role in mounting this challenge.

Till the overthrow of the monarchy in 1958 Iraq remained largely agricultural. It was only after the removal of the puppet king that year that some developmental projects were undertaken. After 1973, reaping the benefits of higher oil prices, welfare expenditues of the state increased considerably. The supply of housing greatly increased, and living standard improved considerably. However, the regime went further, initiating a wide range of projects for industrial diversification, reduction of imports of manufactured goods, increase in agricultural production and reduction of agricultural imports, and a large increase in non-oil exports. Large investments were made in infrastructure, particularly in water projects, roads, railways, and rural electrification. Technical education was greatly expanded, training a generation of qualified personnel for industry.

These measures stood in striking contrast to the Gulf sheikhdoms of Saudi Arabia, Kuwait, and the United Arab Emirates. In those countries, a part of the huge increase in earnings after 1973 was spent on improving the standard of living of the kings' subjects; the rest was invested in foreign banks and foreign treasury bills, principally American. Thus the United States was not fundamentally threatened by the oil price hike: while it paid higher oil prices, most of the extra funds flowed back to its own financial sector. Iraq, by contrast, invested far more of its oil revenues *internally* than other Arab states, and therefore had the most diversified economy among them.

It is worth noting that Iraq's cultural climate and progress in certain areas of social life are abhorred by Islamic fundamentalists. Till 1991, literacy grew rapidly in Iraq, including among women. Iraq is perhaps the freest society in the entire region for women, and women are to be found in several professions.[12]

THE IRAN-IRAQ WAR: SERVING AMERICAN INTERESTS

In 1979, Saddam, already effectively the leader of Iraq, became president and chairman of the Revolutionary Command Council. The entire region stood at a critical juncture.

For one, the pillar of the United States in West Asia, viz., the Pahlavi monarchy in Iran, was overthrown by a massive popular upsurge that Washington was powerless to suppress. This made the United States and its client states deeply anxious at the prospect of similar developments taking place throughout the region.

For another, in Iraq Saddam had drawn on the country's oil wealth to carry out a major military build up, with military expenditures swallowing 8.4 percent of GNP in 1979. Starting in 1958 Iraq had become an increasingly important market for sophisticated Soviet weapons and was considered a member of the Soviet camp. In 1972 Iraq signed a fifteen-year friendship, cooperation and military agreement with the USSR. The Iraqi regime was striving to develop or acquire nuclear weapons. Apart from Israel, the only army in the region to rival Iraq's was Iran's. But after 1979, when the Shah of Iran was overthrown, much of the Iranian army's American equipment became inoperable.

The Iraqi invasion of Iran in 1980 (on the pretext of resolving border disputes) thus solved two major problems for the United States. Over the course of the following decade two of the region's leading military powers, neither of them hitherto friendly to the United States, were tied up in an exhausting conflict with each other. Such conflicts among third world countries create a host of opportunities for imperialist powers to seek new footholds, as happened also in this instance.

Despite its strong ties to the USSR, Iraq turned to the West for support in the war with Iran. This it received massively. As Saddam Hussein later revealed, the United States and Iraq decided to re-establish diplomatic relations—broken off after the 1967 war with Israel—just before Iraq's invasion of Iran in 1980 (the actual implementation was delayed for a few more years in order not to make the linkage too explicit). Diplomatic relations between the United States and Iraq were formally restored in 1984—well after the United States knew, and a UN team confirmed, that Iraq was using chemical weapons against the Iranian troops. (The emissary sent by U.S. president Reagan to negotiate the arrangements was none other than the present U.S. defense secretary, Donald Rumsfeld.) In 1982, the U.S. State Department removed Iraq from its list of 'state sponsors of terrorism,' and fought off efforts by the U.S. Congress to put it back on the list in 1985. Most crucially, the United States blocked condemnation of Iraq's chemical attacks in the UN Security Council. The United States was the sole country to vote against a 1986 Security Council statement condemning Iraq's use of mustard gas against Iranian troops—an atrocity in which it now emerges the United States was directly implicated (as we shall see below).

Brisk trade was done in supplying Iraq. Britain joined France as a major source of weapons for it. Iraq imported uranium from Portugal, France, and Italy, and began constructing centrifuge enrichment facilities with German assistance. The United States arranged massive loans for Iraq's burgeoning war expenditure from American client states such as Kuwait and Saudi Arabia. The U.S. administration provided "crop-spraying" helicopters (to be used for chemical attacks in 1988), let Dow Chemicals ship its chemicals for use on humans, seconded its air force officers to work with their Iraqi counterparts (from 1986), approved technological exports to Iraq's missile procurement agency to extend the missiles' range (1988). In October 1987 and April 1988 U.S. forces themselves attacked Iranian ships and oil platforms.

Militarily, the United States not only provided to Iraq satellite data and information about Iranian military movements, but, as former U.S. Defense Intelligence Agency (DIA) officers have recently revealed to the *New York Times, prepared detailed battle planning for Iraqi forces in this period*[13]—even as Iraq drew worldwide public condemnation for its repeated use of chemical weapons against Iran. According to a senior DIA official, "If Iraq had gone down it would have had a catastrophic effect on Kuwait and Saudi Arabia, and the whole region might have gone down—that was the backdrop of the policy."[14]

One of the battles for which the United States provided battle-planning packages was the Iraqi capture of the strategic Fao peninsula in the Persian Gulf in 1988. Since Iraq eventually relied heavily on mustard gas in the battle, it is clear the United States battle plan tacitly included the use of such weapons. DIA officers undertook a tour of inspection of the Fao peninsula after Iraqi forces successfully retook it, and they reported to their superiors on Iraq's extensive use of chemical weapons, but their superiors were not interested. Col. Walter P. Lang, senior DIA officer at the time, says that "the use of gas on the battlefield by the Iraqis was not a matter of deep strategic concern." The DIA, he claimed, "would have never accepted the use of chemical weapons against civilians, but the use against military objectives was seen as inevitable in the Iraqi struggle for survival." (As we shall see below, chemical weapons were used extensively by the Iraqi army against Kurdish civilians, but DIA officers deny they were "involved in planning any of the military operations in which these assaults occurred.") In the words of another DIA officer, "They [the Iraqis] had gotten better and better" and after a while chemical weapons "were integrated into their fire plan for any large operation." A former participant in the program told the *New York Times* that senior Reagan administration officials did nothing to interfere with the continuation of the program. The Pentagon "wasn't so horrified by Iraq's use of gas," said one veteran of the program. "It was just another way of killing people—whether with a bullet or phosgene, it didn' t make any difference," he said. The recapture of the Fao peninsula was a turning point in the conflict, bringing Iran to the negotiating table.

A U.S. Senate inquiry in 1995 accidentally revealed that during the Iran-Iraq war the United States had sent Iraq samples of all the strains of germs used by the latter to make biological weapons. The strains were sent by the Centers for Disease Control and Prevention [sic] and the American Type Culture Collection to the same sites in Iraq that UN weapons inspectors later determined were part of Iraq's biological weapons program.[15]

It is ironic to hear the United States today talk of Saddam Hussein's attacks on the Kurds in 1988. These attacks had their full support:

As part of the Anfal campaign against the Kurds (February to September 1988), the Iraqi regime used chemical weapons extensively against its own civilian population. Between 50,000 and 186,000 Kurds were killed in these attacks, over 1,200 Kurdish villages were destroyed, and 300,000 Kurds were displaced.... The Anfal campaign was carried out with the acquiescence of the West. Rather than condemn the massacres of Kurds, the United States escalated its support for Iraq. It joined in Iraq's attacks on Iranian facilities, blowing up two Iranian oil rigs and destroying an Iranian frigate a month after the Halabja attack. Within two months, senior U.S. officials were encouraging corporate coordination through an Iraqi state-sponsored forum. The United States administration opposed, and eventually blocked, a U.S. Senate bill that cut off loans to Iraq. The United States approved exports to Iraq of items with dual civilian and military use at double the rate in the aftermath of Halabja as it did before 1988. Iraqi written guarantees about civilian use were accepted by the United States commerce department, which did not request licenses and reviews (as it did for many other countries). The Bush administration approved $695,000 worth of advanced data transmission devices the day before Iraq invaded Kuwait.[16]

The full extent of U.S. complicity in Iraq's "weapons of mass destruction" programs became clear in December 2002, when Iraq submitted an 11,800-page report on these programs to the UN Security Council. The United States insisted on examining the report before anyone else, even before the weapons inspectors, and promptly insisted on removing 8,000 pages from it before allowing the non permanent members of the Security

Council to look at it. Iraq apparently leaked the list of American companies whose names appear in the report to a German daily, *Die Tageszeitung*. Apart from American companies, German firms were heavily implicated. (Saddam Hussein's use of chemical weapons, like his suppression of internal opposition, has been continuously useful to U.S. interests: condoned and abetted during periods of alliance between the two countries, it is routinely exploited for propaganda purposes during periods of tension and war.)

Given this history, we need to understand the strategic and economic aspects of the United States' seemingly inexplicable turnaround on Iraq since 1990.

THE TORMENT OF IRAQ

The Iran-Iraq war formally ended in 1990 with both participants—potentially prosperous and powerful countries—having suffered terrible losses. The "war of the cities" had targeted major population centers and industrial sites on both sides, particularly oil refineries. Iran, lacking the steady flow of sophisticated weapons and American help enjoyed by Iraq, had managed to fight back Iraq's attacks by mobilizing great "human waves" of young volunteers, even teenage boys. While the tactic worked, the cost in lives was enormous. It was the apprehension of an internal uprising that led the Iranian leaders to come to terms with Iraq after the fall of the Fao peninsula in 1988.

Iraq's economy, too, badly needed rebuilding. Developmental programs had been neglected for the previous decade. Exploration and development of the country's fabulous oil resources had stagnated. To pay for the war, the country had accumulated an $80 billion foreign debt—more than half of that owed to the Gulf states. Having nothing to show for the terrible price of the war, Iraq's rulers were desperate.

An Opportunity for the United States

For the United States, however, this catastrophe for the two countries was a satisfactory situation, and held promise of much greater gains. The exhausted Iran was no longer a major threat to American interests in the rest of the region. *And, as we shall see, Iraq's unstable situation was creating conditions for the United States to achieve a vital objective: permanent installation of its military in West Asia.* Direct control over West Asian oil resources—the world's richest and most cheaply accessible—would allow the United States to manipulate oil supplies and prices according to its strategic interests, and thereby consolidate American global supremacy against any future challenger. (This aspect has been dealt with in a separate article in this issue.)

The world situation was favorable to such a plan. The Soviet Union was on the verge of collapse, and would be unable to prevent American intervention in the region. Nor would European, Japanese, or Chinese reservations be of much consequence. The real hurdle was the opposition of the Arab *masses* to any such presence of U.S. troops—even more to their permanent installation.

What was required, then, was a credible pretext for U.S. intervention and continuing presence.

Shock to Iraq

After the close U.S.-Iraq collaboration during the 1980–1990 Iran-Iraq war described above, it is hardly surprising that Saddam Hussein expected some sort of compensation from the West for his war with Iran, and felt confident that his demands would be given a sympathetic hearing. Given that the war was projected by the West and the Gulf states (Kuwait, the United Arab Emirates, and Saudi Arabia) to be a defensive action against Iran's overrunning the entire region, Saddam assumed not only that Iraq's debt to the Gulf states would be forgiven, but indeed that those states would help with the desperately needed reconstruction of the Iraqi economy.

Instead the opposite occurred. U.S. client regimes such as Kuwait, Saudi Arabia, and the United Arab Emirates began hiking their production of oil, thus prolonging the collapse in oil prices that began in 1986. This had a devastating impact on war-torn Iraq. Oil constituted half Iraq's GDP and the bulk of government revenues, so a collapse in oil prices was catastrophic for the Iraqi economy. It would also curb Iraq's rearming.

A further, remarkable development was Kuwait's theft of oil from Rumaila field by slant-drilling (drilling at an angle, instead of straight down) near the border. (The Rumaila field lies almost entirely inside Iraq.) Given that Kuwait is itself oil-rich, the theft of Iraq's oil appears a deliberate provocation. It is worth keeping in mind that Iraq already had not only specific border disputes with Kuwait but had from time to time advanced a claim to the whole of Kuwait.[17] In this light it is difficult to imagine that small, lightly armed Kuwait would have carried out such provocative acts as slant-drilling the territory of well-armed Iraq without a go-ahead from the United States.

Saddam's Plea

It appears that Saddam believed he could threaten invasion of, or actually invade, Kuwait as a bargaining chip to achieve his demands—in particular the forgiveness of loans and a curb on the Gulf states' oil production. The transcript of Saddam's conversation with the United States ambassador to Baghdad, April Glaspie, just a week before the Iraqi invasion of Kuwait in 1990, is revealing of the relation between the two states. Saddam does not emerge as a megalomaniac, nor does he stress Iraq's historical and legal claims to Kuwait. Rather, he emphasizes his financial needs. He pleads for American understanding by pointing explicitly to Iraq's services to the United States and its client states in the region:

> The decision to establish relations with the U.S. [was] taken in 1980 during the two months prior to the war between us and Iran. When the war started, and to avoid misinterpretation, we postponed the establishment of relations hoping that the war would end soon. But because the war lasted for a long time, and to emphasize the fact that we are a non aligned country [i.e., not part of the Soviet bloc], it was important to re-establish relations with the United States. And we choose to do this in 1984.... When relations were re-established we hoped for a better understanding and for better cooperation.... We dealt with each other during the war and we had dealings on various levels....

Iraq came out of the war burdened with $40 billion debts, excluding the aid given by Arab states, some of whom consider that too to be a debt, although they knew—and you knew too—that without Iraq they would not have had these sums and the future of the region would have been entirely different. We began to face the policy of the drop in the price of oil.... The price at one stage had dropped to $12 a barrel and a reduction in the modest Iraqi budget of $6 billion to $7 billion is a disaster....

We had hoped that soon the American authorities would make the correct decision regarding their relations with Iraq.... But when planned and deliberate policy forces the price of oil down without good commercial reasons, then that means another war against Iraq. Because military war kills people by bleeding them, and economic war kills their humanity by depriving them of their chance to have a good standard of living.... Kuwait and the U.A.E. were at the front of this policy aimed at lowering Iraq's position and depriving its people of higher economic standards. And you know that our relations with the Emirates and Kuwait had been good....

I have read the American statements speaking of friends in the area. Of course, it is the right of everyone to choose their friends. We can have no objections. But you know you are not the ones who pro-tected your friends during the war with Iran. I assure you, had the Iranians overrun the region, the American troops would not have stopped them, except by the use of nuclear weapons.... Yours is a soci-ety which cannot accept 10,000 dead in one battle. You know that Iran agreed to the cease-fire not because the United States had bombed one of the oil platforms after the liberation of the Fao. Is this Iraq's reward for its role in securing the stability of the region and for protecting it from an unknown flood?...

It is not reasonable to ask our people to bleed rivers of blood for eight years then to tell them, "Now you have to accept aggression from Kuwait, the U.A.E., or from the U.S. or from Israel."... We do not place America among the enemies. We place it where we want our friends to be and we try to be friends. But repeated American statements last year make it apparent that America did not regard us as friends.[18]

Calculated Response

Without the fact of America's intentions mentioned earlier, Glaspie's response to Saddam's statements would be puzzling. The conversation took place even as Iraq had massed troops at the Kuwaiti border and declared that it considered Kuwait's acts to be aggression: *it was plain to the world that Iraq was about to invade.* Given the later American response, one would have expected that, a week before the invasion, the United States would send a clear message that the United States *response to an invasion would be military intervention.* Instead the United States ambassador responded in the mildest possible terms ("concern"), emphasizing that:

We have no opinion on the Arab-Arab conflicts, like your border disagreement with Kuwait. I was in the American Embassy in Kuwait during the late '60s. The instruction we had during this period was that we should express no opinion on this issue and that the issue is not associated with America. James Baker has directed our official spokesmen to emphasize this instruction.

We hope you can solve this problem using any suitable methods via Klibi or via President Mubarak. All that we hope is that these issues are solved quickly. With regard to all of this, can I ask you to see how the issue appears to us? My assessment after 25 years' service in this area is that your objective must have strong backing from your Arab brothers. I now speak of oil. But you, Mr. President, have fought through a horrific and painful war. Frankly, we can see only that you have deployed massive troops in the south. Normally that would not be any of our business. But when this happens in the context of what you said on your national day, then when we read the details in the two letters of the Foreign Minister, then when we see the Iraqi point of view that the measures taken by the U.A.E. and Kuwait is, in the final analysis, parallel to military aggression against Iraq, then it would be reasonable for me to be concerned. And for this reason, I received an instruction to ask you, in the spirit of friendship—not in the spirit of confrontation—regarding your intentions.[19]

This clearly indicated that while the United States would show "concern" at any invasion, it would maintain a distance and treat the matter as a dispute between Arab states, to be resolved by negotiation. Thus Saddam badly misread America's real intentions. His invasion of Kuwait, a sovereign state and a member of the UN, provided the United States with the opportunity swiftly to mobilise the UN Security Council and form a worldwide coalition against Iraq. Crucially, his invasion of an Arab state created a situation where a number of Arab states, such as Egypt, Syria, and Saudi Arabia could join the coalition.[20]

Peaceful Withdrawal a "Nightmare Scenario"

UN Security Council Resolution 661, passed in August 1990, demanded immediate and unconditional withdrawal from Kuwait, and imposed sanctions on Iraq. Sanctions were tried only for as long as it took for the United States to build up enough troops in the region and secure international financing for the war effort. In November 1990, the United States got UN Security Council Resolution 678 passed, providing for the use of "all necessary means" to end the occupation of Kuwait.[21] The United States scotched all diplomatic efforts by the USSR, Europe, and Arab countries by continuing to insist that Iraq withdraw unconditionally.

A last-minute proposal was made by the French that Iraq would withdraw if the United States agreed to convene an international conference on peace in the region (this would include discussion of the continued illegal occupation by Israel of the West Bank, Gaza, and the Golan Heights, the subject of the unenforced UN Security Council Resolution 242, as well as Iraq's occupation at the time of south Lebanon). However, this too was shot down by the United States and Britain. In December 1990, the press tellingly quoted U.S. officials saying that a peaceful Iraqi withdrawal was a "nightmare scenario."[22]

"Fish in a Barrel"[23]

The colossal scale and merciless tactics of the 1991 assault on Iraq suggest that U.S. war aims greatly exceeded the UN-endorsed mission of expelling Saddam from Kuwait. The military power arrayed and employed by the U.S., Britain, and their allies was grotesquely disproportionate to Iraqi defenses. Evidently, the intent was to punish Iraq so severely as to create an unforgettable object lesson for any nation contemplating defiance of U.S. wishes. The Gulf war's aerial bombing campaign was the most savage since Vietnam. During 43 days of war, the U.S. flew 109,876 sorties and dropped 84,200 tons of bombs.[24] Average monthly tonnage of ordnance used nearly equaled that of World War II, but the resulting destruction was far more efficient due to better technology and the feebleness of Iraq's anti aircraft defenses.[25]

While war raged, the United States military carefully managed press briefings in order to suggest that the bombing raids were surgical strikes against purely military targets, made possible by a new generation of precision-guided "smart weapons." The reality was far different. Ninety-three percent of munitions used by the allies consisted of unguided "dumb" bombs, dropped primarily by Vietnam-era B-52 carpet bombers. About 70 percent of bombs and missiles missed their targets, frequently destroying private homes and killing civilians.[26] The United States also made devastating use of anti personnel weapons, including fuel-air explosives and 15,000-pound "daisy-cutter" bombs (conventional explosives capable of causing destruction equivalent to a nuclear attack—also used by the United States in Afghanistan); the petroleum-based incendiary napalm (which was used to incinerate entrenched Iraqi soldiers); and 61,000 cluster bombs from which were strewn 20 million "bomblets," which continue to kill Iraqis to this day.[27]

Predictably, this style of warfare resulted in massive civilian casualties. In one well-remembered incident, as many as four hundred men, women, and children were killed at one blow when, in apparent indifference to the Geneva Conventions, the United States targeted a civilian air raid shelter in the Ameriyya district of western Baghdad. Thousands died in similar fashion due to daylight raids in heavily populated residential areas and business districts throughout the country.[28] According to a UN estimate, as many as 15,000 civilians died as a direct result of allied bombing.[29]

Meanwhile, between 100,000 and 200,000 Iraqi soldiers lost their lives in what can literally be described as massive overkill.[30] The heaviest toll appears to have been inflicted by U.S. carpet bombing of Iraqi positions near the Kuwait-Iraq border, where tens of thousands of ill-fed, ill-equipped conscripts were helplessly pinned down in trenches. Most were desperate to surrender as the ground war began, but advancing allied forces had little use for prisoners. Thousands were buried alive as tanks equipped with plows and bulldozers smashed through earthwork defenses and rolled over foxholes.[31]

Others were cut down ruthlessly as they tried to surrender or flee. "It's like someone turned on the kitchen light on late at night, and the cockroaches started scurrying. We finally got them out where we can find them and kill them," remarked Air Force Colonel Dick "Snake" White.[32] According to John Balzar of the *Los Angeles Times,* infrared films of the United States assault suggested "sheep, flushed from a pen—Iraqi infantry soldiers bewildered and terrified, jarred from sleep and fleeing their bunkers under a hell storm of fire. One by one they were cut down by attackers they couldn't see or understand. Some were literally blown to bits by bursts of 30mm exploding cannon shells."[33]

Since resistance was futile and surrender potentially fatal, Iraqi soldiers deserted whenever possible. By February 26, Saddam acknowledged the inevitable and ordered his troops to withdraw from Kuwait. Surviving soldiers commandeered vehicles of every description and fled homeward.

Although an overwhelming victory already been achieved, U.S. and British forces staged a merciless attack on the retreating and defenseless Iraqi troops. The resulting massacre, immediately dubbed the "Turkey Shoot" by U.S. soldiers, took place along a 60-mile stretch of highway leading from Kuwait to Basra, where U.S. planes cut off the long convoys at either end and proceeded to strafe and firebomb the trapped vehicles. Many thousands, including untold numbers of civilian refugees, were blown apart or incinerated. "It was like shooting fish in a barrel," said one U.S. pilot.[34]

Behind the Systematic Destruction of Iraq's Civilian Infrastructure

The bombing of Iraq began on January 16, 1991. Far from restricting themselves to evicting Iraq from Kuwait, or attacking only military targets, the U.S.-led coalition's bombing campaign systematically destroyed Iraq's civilian infrastructure, including electricity generation, communication, water and sanitation facilities. *For more than a month the bombing of Iraq continued without any attempt to send in troops for the purported purpose of Operation Desert Storm;* namely, to evict Iraqi troops from Kuwait.

That the United States was quite clear about the consequences of such a bombing campaign is evident from intelligence documents now being declassified. "Iraq Water Treatment Vulnerabilities," dated 22 January 1991 (a week after the war began) provides the rationale for the attack on Iraq's water supply treatment capabilities: "Iraq depends on importing specialized equipment and some chemicals to purify its water supply.... With no domestic sources of both water treatment replacement parts and some essential chemicals, Iraq will continue attempts to circumvent United Nations sanctions to import these vital commodities. Failing to secure supplies will result in a shortage of pure drinking water for much of the population. This could lead to increased incidences, if not epidemics, of disease." Imports of chlorine, the document notes, had been placed under embargo, and "recent reports indicate that the chlorine supply is critically low." A "loss of water treatment capability" was already in evidence, and though there was no danger of a "precipitous halt" it would probably take six months or more for the system to be "fully degraded."

Even more explicitly, the U.S. Defense Intelligence Agency wrote a month later: "Conditions are favorable for communicable disease outbreaks, particularly in major urban areas affected by coalition bombing.... Current public health problems are attributable to the reduction of normal preventive medicine, waste disposal, water purification/distribution, electricity, and decreased ability to control disease outbreaks. Any urban area in Iraq that has received infrastructure damage will have similar problems."[35]

In the south of Iraq, the United States fired more than one million rounds (more than 340 tons in all) of munitions tipped with radioactive uranium. This later resulted in a major increase in health problems such as cancer and deformities. While the United States has not admitted any linkage between its use of depleted uranium (DU) shells and such health problems, European governments, investigating complaints from their veterans in the NATO attack on Yugoslavia, have confirmed widespread radiation contamination in Kosovo as a result of the use of DU shells there.

Manipulation to Justify Partial Occupation

During the conflict, the United States decided not to march to Baghdad, and decided instead to stop on the outskirts of Basra and Nasriyya. Evidently, the United States hoped that the defeat would result in Saddam being replaced in a coup by a pro-U.S. strongman from the same ruling circles. (The stability of such a regime would require the preservation of Saddam's elite military force, the Republican Guard, which was massed in defensive positions outside Baghdad at war's end.) The United States was uncertain of the political forces that would be unleashed in any other scenario. For example, the United States feared southern Iraq, predominantly Shiite, would come under Iranian influence if it seceded. Formal independence for Kurdish regions in the north of Iraq would destabilize the northern neighbor, the important U.S. client state Turkey, which brutally suppresses the demand of its large Kurdish population for independence.

While George Bush Sr., then president, instigated a rebellion in southern Iraq with his calls to the people to "take matters into their own hands," when the rising actually took place, the massive U.S. occupying force still stationed in the region remained a mute spectator to its suppression. Similarly, when Iraqi forces chased Kurdish rebels in the north to the Turkish border, Turkey prevented their entry.

American complicity in these two developments was designed so that these developments could be cynically manipulated by the United States to justify a permanent infringement of Iraq's sovereignty. The UN Security Council Resolution 688 of April 1991 demanded Iraq "cease this repression" of its minorities, but did not call for its enforcement by military action. The United States and Britain nevertheless used UNSC 688 to justify the enforcement of what it called "no-fly zones," whereby Iraqi planes are not allowed to fly over the north and south of the country (north of the 36th parallel, and south of the 32nd parallel). These zones are enforced by U.S.-U.K. patrols and *almost daily bombings*. After the withdrawal of UN weapons inspectors in 1998, the average monthly release of bombs rose dramatically from. 025 tons to five tons. U.S. and UK planes could now target any part of what the United States considered the Iraqi air defense system.[36] Between 1991 and 2000 U.S. and U.K. fighter planes flew more than 280,000 sorties. UN officials have documented that these bombings routinely hit civilians and essential civilian infrastructure, as well as livestock.[37]

Sanctions: Genocide

After the war, Iraq remained under the comprehensive regime of sanctions placed by the UN in 1990. These sanctions were to last until Iraq fulfilled UNSC 687—elimination of its programs for developing chemical, biological, and nuclear weapons, dismantling of its long-range missiles, a system of inspections to verify compliance, acceptance of a UN-demarcated Iraq-Kuwait border, payment of war compensation, and the return of Kuwaiti property and prisoners of war. Since the verification of compliance was bound to be a drawn-out and controversy-ridden process, the sanctions could be prolonged indefinitely.

The result has been catastrophic—the greatest among the catastrophes of that decade of great economic catastrophes worldwide. By 1993, the Iraqi economy under the crunch of sanctions shrank to *one-fifth* of its size in 1979, and shrank further in 1994. Rations lasted only about one-third to half of a month.[38]

Although "humanitarian goods" were excluded from the embargo, the embargo had not clearly defined such goods, which had to be cleared by the UN sanctions committee. Later, in order to deflect growing criticism of the sanctions and in order to preempt French and Russian counter proposals, the U.K. and U.S. introduced UNSC 986. By this resolution proceeds from Iraq's oil sales would go into a UN-controlled account; and Iraq could place orders for humanitarian goods—to be scrutinized by the UN Security Council.

The United States tried to limit the definition of "humanitarian goods" to food and medicine alone, preventing the import of items needed to restore water supply, sanitation, electrical power, even medical facilities. Among the items kept out by American veto, on the grounds that they might have a military application, were chemicals, laboratory equipment, generators, communications equipment, ambulances (on the pretext that they contain communications equipment), chlorinators, and even pencils (on the pretext that they contain graphite, which has military uses).[39] The United States and Britain placed "holds" on $5.3 billion worth of goods in early 2002 alone.[40] Even this does not tell the full impact, since the item held back often renders imports of other parts useless.

The *Economist* (London), although an eager supporter of U.S. policies toward Iraq, described conditions in the besieged country by 2000:

Sanctions impinge on the lives of all Iraqis every moment of the day. In Basra, Iraq's second city, power flickers on and off, unpredictable in the hours it is available.... Smoke from jerry-rigged generators and vehicles hangs over the town in a thick cloud. The tap-water causes diarrhea, but few can afford the bottled sort. Because the sewers have broken down, pools of stinking muck have leached through the surface all over town. That effluent, combined with pollution upstream, has killed most of the fish in the Shatt al-Arab river and has left the remainder unsafe to eat. The government can no longer spray for sand flies or mosquitoes, so insects have proliferated, along with the diseases they carry.

Most of the once-elaborate array of government services have vanished. The archaeological service has taken to burying painstakingly excavated ruins for want of the proper preservative chemicals. The government-maintained irrigation and drainage network has crumbled, leaving much of Iraq's prime agricultural land either too dry or too salty to cultivate. Sheep and cattle, no longer shielded by government vaccination programs, have succumbed to pests and diseases by the hundreds of thousands. Many teachers in the state-run schools do not bother to show up for work anymore. Those who do must teach listless, malnourished children, often without the benefit of books, desks or even black-boards.[41]

During the first three years of the oil-for-food regime, the annual ceiling placed by the UN was just $170 per Iraqi. Out of this meager sum a further $51 was deducted and diverted to the UN Compensation Commission, which any government, organization, or individual who claimed to have suffered as a result of Iraq's attack on Kuwait could approach for compensation. (Within the remaining sum, a disproportionate amount is diverted under U.S. direction to the Kurdish north—with 13 percent of the population but 20 percent of the funds—because this region is no longer ruled by Baghdad. The cynical intention is to point to improved conditions in this favored region as proof that it is not the sanctions but Saddam that is responsible for Iraqi suffering.) Later, the UN removed the ceiling on Iraq's oil earnings—but prevented the rehabilitation of the Iraqi oil industry, thus ensuring that in effect the ceiling remained.

In 1998, the UN carried out a nationwide survey of health and nutrition. It found that mortality rates among children under five in central and southern Iraq had doubled from the previous decade. *That would suggest 500,000 excess deaths of children by 1998.* Excess deaths of children continue at the rate of 5,000 a month. UNICEF estimated in 2002 that 70 percent of child deaths in Iraq result from diarrhea and acute respiratory infections. This is the result—as foretold accurately by U.S. intelligence in 1991—of the breakdown of systems to provide clean water, sanitation, and electrical power. Adults, too, particularly the elderly and other vulnerable sections, have succumbed. The overall toll, of all ages, was put at *1.2 million* in a 1997 UNICEF report.

The evidence of the effect of the sanctions came from the most authoritative sources. Denis Halliday, UN humanitarian coordinator in Iraq from 1997 to 1998, resigned in protest against the operation of the sanctions, which he termed deliberate *"genocide."* He was replaced by Hans von Sponeck, who resigned in 2000, on the same grounds. Jutta Burghardt, director of the UN World Food Program operation in Iraq, also resigned, saying, "I fully support what Mr. von Sponeck was saying."

There is no room for doubt that genocide was conscious U.S. policy. On May 12, 1996, U.S. Secretary of State Madeleine Albright was asked by Lesley Stahl of CBS television: "We have heard that half a million children have died. I mean, that's more than died in Hiroshima. And, you know, is the price worth it?" Albright replied: "I think this is a very hard choice, but the price, we think the price is worth it."

RETURN OF IMPERIALIST OCCUPATION

"Weapons Inspection" as Tool of Provocation, Spying, Assassination

There can also be no doubt now that UNSCOM, the UN weapons inspections body, was made into a tool of the U.S. mission to take over Iraq. Not only did UNSCOM coordinate consistently with U.S. and Israeli intelligence on which sites to inspect, but agents of these services were placed in the inspection teams. Scott Ritter, former UN weapons inspector, writes:

> I recall during my time as a chief inspector in Iraq the dozens of extremely fit "missile experts" and "logistics specialists" who frequented my inspection teams and others. Drawn from U.S. units such as Delta Force or from CIA paramilitary teams such as the Special Activities Staff, these specialists had a legitimate part to play in the difficult cat-and-mouse effort to disarm Iraq. So did the teams of British radio intercept operators I ran in Iraq from 1996 to 1998— which listened in on the conversations of Hussein's inner circle—and the various other intelligence specialists who were part of the inspection effort. The presence of such personnel on inspection teams was, and is, viewed by the Iraqi government as an unacceptable risk to its nation's security. As early as 1992, the Iraqis viewed the teams I led inside Iraq as a threat to the safety of their president.[42]

Rolf Ekeus, who led the weapons inspections mission from 1991 to 1997, revealed in a recent interview to Swedish radio that he knew what was up: "*There is no doubt that the Americans wanted to influence inspections to further certain fundamental U.S. interests.*" The United States pressure included attempts to "create crises in relations with Iraq, which to some extent was linked to the overall political situation—internationally but also perhaps nationally.... There was an ambition to cause a crisis through pressure for, shall we say, blunt provocation, for example by inspection of the Department of Defense, which at least from an Iraqi point of view must have been provocative." He said that *the United States had wanted information about how Iraq's security services were organized and what its conventional military capacity was. And he said he was "conscious" of the United States seeking information on where President Saddam Hussein was hiding, "which could be of interest if one were to target him personally."*[43]

By 1997, Ekeus reported to the Security Council that 93 percent of Iraq's major weapons capability had been destroyed. UNSCOM and the International Atomic Energy Agency (IAEA) certified that Iraq's nuclear stocks were gone and most of its long-range systems had been destroyed. (IAEA inspectors continue to date to travel to Iraq, and report full compliance.) In 1999 a special panel of the Security Council recorded that Iraq's main biological weapons facility (whose stocks were supplied, as mentioned earlier, by the United States) had "been destroyed and rendered harmless." Pressure began to build, especially from Russia and France—for reasons we will mention later—for the step-by-step lifting of sanctions, or at least clarity on what action by Iraq would lead to the lifting of sanctions.

Iraq's fulfilment of UNSC 687 was seen by the United States as a threat to its continuing plans to strip Iraq of its tattered sovereignty. Ekeus was replaced in 1997 by the Australian Richard Butler, who owed his post to American support and paid scant heed to the other members of the Security Council. After a series of confrontational attempts to inspect sites such as the defense ministry and the presidential palaces, Butler complained of non-cooperation by the Iraqis and withdrew his inspectors in November and December 1998, the second time without bothering to consult the Security Council—apart from the United States. This was in preparation for Operation Desert Fox—torrential bombing by the United States and Britain throughout southern and central Iraq from December 16 to 19, 1998. Significantly, the United States and U.K. did not bother to consult the Security Council before carrying out this action.

The Big Prize

Apart from the terrible direct human impact of the sanctions, it is important to bear in mind another calculation of the United States in prolonging the sanctions until it invades: as long as the sanctions stay, foreign investment in Iraq cannot take place, nor rehabilitation of the country's oil industry. *Sanctions are thus an important instrument for the United States to prevent other imperialist powers from getting a foothold in Iraq—* recalling an earlier theme of Iraqi history.

Iraq's oil resources are vast, surpassed only by Saudi Arabia, and as cheap to extract as Saudi oil. The country's 115 billion barrels of proven oil reserves are matched by perhaps an equal quantity yet to be explored. "Since no geological survey has been conducted in Iraq since the 1970s, experts believe that the proven reserves underestimate the country's actual oil wealth, which could be as large as 250 billion barrels. Three decades of political instability and war have kept Iraq from developing 55 of its 70 proven oil fields. Eight of these fields could harbor more than a billion barrels each of "easy oil" which is close to the surface and inexpensive to extract.[44] "There is nothing like it anywhere else in the world," says Gerald Butt, Gulf editor of the *Middle East Economic Survey*. "It's the big prize."[45]

Iraq's pre-war production was three million barrels a day and present production capacity is put at 2.8 million barrels a day. In fact, because of deteriorating equipment, it is hard put to reach that figure, and it currently exports less than a million barrels a day. It is estimated that, with adequate investment, Iraq's production can reach seven to eight million barrels a day within five years. That compares with Saudi Arabia's current production of 7.1 million barrels a day, close to 10 percent of world consumption.

This expansion of Iraqi production is impossible as long as the sanctions stay in place. The UN warned in 2000 of a "major breakdown" in Iraq's oil industry if spare parts and equipment were not forthcoming. The

United States said any extra money should only be used "for short-term improvements to the Iraqi oil industry and not to make long-term repairs." The United States Department of Energy said: "As of early January, 2002, the head of the UN Iraq program, Benon Sevan, expressed 'grave concern' at the volume of 'holds' put on contracts for oil field development, and stated the entire program was threatened with paralysis. According to Sevan, these holds amounted to nearly 2000 contracts worth about $5 billion, about 80 percent of which were 'held' by the United States."[46]

From the point of view of U.S. oil interests, then, the sanctions are a double-edged sword: even as they keep international competition temporarily at bay, they preclude the exploitation of oil reserves with an estimated value of several trillion dollars. The war against Saddam Hussein is intended, among other things, to resolve this contradiction.

In June 2001, France and Russia proposed in the Security Council to remove restrictions on foreign investment in the Iraqi oil industry.[47] However, the United States and U.K. predictably killed the proposal. American companies are barred by American law from investing in Iraq, and so all the contracts for development of Iraqi fields have been cornered by companies from other countries. The *Wall Street Journal* compiled the following information from oil industry sources:

Companies That Initiated Deals with Iraq in the 1990s, and Reserves of the Fields They Would Drill If Sanctions Are Lifted:[48]

COMPANY	COUNTRY	RESERVES (billion barrels)
Elf Aquitaine*	France	9-20
Lukoil, Zarubezneft Mashinoimport	Russia	7.5-15
Total SA*	France	3.5-7
China Nat'l Petroleum	China	under 2
ENI/Agip	Italy	under 2

now part of TotalFinaElf

Lukoil's contract to drill the West Qurna field is valued at $20 billion, and Zarubezneft's concession to develop the bin Umar field is put at up to $90 billion. The total value of Iraq's foreign contract awards could reach *$1.1 trillion*, according to the International Energy Agency's *World Energy Outlook*.[49]

One of the major objectives of the United States' impending invasion of Iraq is to nullify these agreements. "The concern of my government," a Russian official at the UN told the *Observer* in October 2002, "is that the concessions agreed upon between Baghdad and numerous enterprises will be reneged upon, and that U.S. companies will enter to take the greatest share of those existing contracts.... Yes, if you could say it that way—an oil grab by Washington."[50]

France, too, fears "suffering economically from U.S. oil ambitions at the end of a war." But it may nevertheless back the invasion: "Government sources say they fear—existing concessions aside—France could be cut out of the spoils if it did not support the war and show a significant military presence. If it comes to war, France is determined to be allotted a more prestigious role in the fighting than in the 1991 Gulf war, when its main role was to occupy lightly defended ground. Negotiations have been going on between the state-owned TotalFinaElf company and the United States about redistribution of oil regions between the world's major oil companies."[51]

The "oil grab" was made explicit by former CIA director R. James Woolsey in an interview with the *Washington Post*: "France and Russia have oil companies and interests in Iraq. They should be told that if they are of assistance in moving Iraq toward decent government, we'll do the best we can to ensure that the new government and American companies work closely with them." But he added: "If they throw in their lot with Saddam, it will be difficult to the point of impossible to persuade the new Iraqi government to work with them."[52]

Ahmed Chalabi, the leader of the London-based "Iraqi National Congress," which enjoys the tactical (and probably temporary) support of the Bush administration but virtually none in Iraq, met executives of three U.S. multinationals in October in Washington to negotiate the carving up of Iraq's oil reserves after the U. S. invasion. Chalabi told the *Washington Post* : "American companies will have a big shot at Iraqi oil."[53] He favored the creation of a U.S.-led consortium to develop Iraq's fields. So stark is American dominance that even Lord Browne, the head of BP (formerly known as British Petroleum) warned that "British oil companies have been squeezed out of postwar Iraq even before the first shot has been fired in any U.S.-led land invasion."[54]

The Logic of Invasion

Given this logic, it is hardly surprising that Bush and his cabinet were planning the invasion of Iraq even before he came to office in January 2001. The plan was drawn up by a right-wing think tank for Dick Cheney, now vice president, Donald Rumsfeld, defense secretary, Paul Wolfowitz, Rumsfeld's deputy, Bush's younger brother Jeb Bush, and Lewis Libby, Cheney's chief of staff. As Neil Mackay notes, the plan shows that Bush's cabinet intended to take military control of the Gulf region whether or not Saddam Hussein was in power:

> The United States has for decades sought to play a more permanent role in Gulf regional security. While the unresolved conflict with Iraq provides the immediate justification, *the need for a substantial American force presence in the Gulf transcends the issue of the regime of Saddam Hussein.*[55]

Another report prepared in April 2001 for Cheney by an institute run by James Baker (U.S. secretary of state under George Bush Sr.) ran along similar lines: "Iraq remains a destabilizing influence ... in the flow of oil to international markets from the Middle East. Saddam Hussein has also demonstrated a willingness to use the oil weapon and to use his own export program to manipulate oil markets." The report complains that Iraq "turns its taps on and off when it has felt such action was in its strategic interest to do so," adding that there is a "possibility that Saddam Hussein may remove Iraqi oil from the market for an extended period of time" in order to damage prices. The report recommends that "therefore the United States should conduct an immediate policy review toward Iraq including military, energy, economic, and political/diplomatic assessments." The report was an important input for the national energy plan—the "Cheney Report"—formulated by the American vice president and released by the White House in early May 2001. The Cheney Report calls for a major increase in U.S. engagement in regions such as the Persian Gulf in order to secure future petroleum supplies.

Within hours of the attacks of September 11, with no evidence pointing at Iraq's involvement in the attacks, U.S. defense secretary Rumsfeld ordered the military to begin working on strike plans. Notes of the meeting quote Rumsfeld as saying he wanted "best info fast. Judge whether good enough to hit S.H. [meaning Saddam Hussein] at the same time. Not only UBL [the initials used to identify Usama bin Laden]." The notes quote Rumsfeld as saying. "Go massive. Sweep it all up. Things related and not."

The Revival of Old Themes

At the start of the twenty-first century, then, broad themes of Iraqi history from the first half of the twentieth century return: imperialist invasion and occupation to grab the region's resources, and rivalries between different imperialist powers as they strain for the prize.

Yet we ought not to forget another major theme from Iraqi history: the anti-imperialist resistance of the Iraqi masses. Even the most jaundiced Western correspondent reporting from Baghdad has been struck by how today Saddam Hussein has become, for the Iraqi people, a symbol of their defiance of American imperialism. Indeed, he has become a symbol of such defiance for the entire Arab people.

The hour of the invasion draws near. As we write this, on December 28, 2002, the Iraqi government has told a solidarity conference in Baghdad that "he who attacks our country will lose. We will fight from village to village, from city to city and from street to street in every city.... Iraq's oil, nationalized by the president ... from the hands of the British and the Americans in 1972... will remain in the hands of this people and this leadership."

The Iraqi armed forces may not be able to put up extended resistance to the onslaught. But the Iraqi people have not buckled to American dictates for the past more than eleven years of torment. They will not meekly surrender to the imminent American-led military occupation of their country. And that fact itself carries grave consequences for American imperialism's broader designs.

3. The Real Reasons for the U.S. Invasion of Iraq—and Beyond

The United States' current strategic agenda is of staggering propor-
tions. It is not secret: it is being discussed openly in the American
press and academia; various documents reflecting it, official and
semi official, are in circulation; and the United States is implementing that
agenda at breakneck speed. By the time this book is published, the United
States will have begun its bombing and invasion of Iraq, the second third
world country to be attacked in less than two years.

On the face of it, current American plans, as outlined below, are so
sweeping and ambitious as to be adventurist and untenable. However, we will
attempt below to show that there is a logic behind these measures, flowing
from the condition of the U.S. economy and its place in the world economy.

Given the massive imbalance of forces, the immediate military success
of the current U.S. mission is not in doubt. But its medium- and long-
term prospects hinge not only on the United States' unrivaled military
strength but on three other factors: the United States' own underlying economic condition, which is weakening; the position of other imperialist
powers, which is tenuously balanced and may turn into active opposition;
and the stance of the world's people—growing conscious opposition in
the advanced world and, crucially, popular explosions and resistance battles in the targeted third world.

The Current Strategic Agenda of the United States

To sum up the following account: The United States plans a massive
expansionist drive around the world (and indeed even in outer space). In
this it plans to take full advantage of its overwhelming military suprema-

cy, including hitherto impermissible means, with inevitably terrible effects on the targeted populations. Not only inconvenient regimes but even certain U.S. client regimes (such as Saudi Arabia) may be targeted. These countries are slated for direct rule by the American military, or rule under close and detailed direction by U.S. monitors—encompassing not only foreign policy and economic policy, but political, social and cultural institutions as well. Direct control of oil will pass into American hands. Importantly, this drive is intended to prevent the emergence of rivals to American worldwide hegemony.

The first part of the following account draws on reports produced by private U.S. bodies as well as press reports. We do not suggest that all the "grand strategies" and schemes mentioned therein have been *finalized*. The United States ruling classes generally adopt a drawn-out process in the course of which they reconcile and resolve the often conflicting demands of their own various sections. Typically, apart from legislators and the press, a proliferation of research institutes, semi-governmental bodies, and academic forums circulate proposals voicing the case of one or the other lobby (leaving the administration free to deny that they constitute official policy). These proposals elicit objections from other sections, through similar media; other powerful countries press their interests, directly or indirectly; and the entire discussion, in the light of the strength of the respective interests, helps shape the course of action finally adopted and helps coalesce the various ruling class sections around it. (This process, of course, has nothing to do with democratic debate, since the *people* are excluded as participants, and are included only as a factor to be taken into account.)

The welter of "secret" reports, private discussions, and briefings by unnamed official sources being reported in the press are part of this process. Keeping these qualifications in mind, these reports offer an invaluable window into the current policy of the American ruling classes.

"Project for the New American Century"

Months before George W. Bush assumed office in January 2001, a report was drawn up by a group called Project for the New American Century

(PNAC). The driving force behind the group was Richard Perle, a member of the Reagan administration, member of the board of extreme right-wing think tanks such as the American Enterprise Institute and the Hudson Institute, and currently the head of the Defense Policy Board, an advisory group to the Pentagon. Other founders of the PNAC also now occupy leading positions in the Bush administration: Dick Cheney, now vice president, Donald Rumsfeld, defense secretary, Paul Wolfowitz, deputy defense secretary, I. Lewis Libby, Cheney's chief of staff, William J. Bennett, Reagan's education secretary, and Zalmay Khalilzad, American special envoy to Afghanistan and imminently to the "free Iraqi people." (Governor Jeb Bush, George's younger brother, was also among the founders.) Hence the report reflects the intentions of those now in office.

Titled "Rebuilding America's Defenses: Strategy, Forces, and Resources for a New Century," the report spells out "American grand strategy" for "as far into the future as possible"—the project's reference to the new American "century" presumably demarcating the outer boundary. Among its highlights are the following:

- "The United States has for decades sought to play a more permanent role in Gulf regional security. *While the unresolved conflict with Iraq provides the immediate justification, the need for a substantial American force presence in the Gulf transcends the issue of the regime of Saddam Hussein*" (emphasis added). Clearly, the American plan to invade Iraq has nothing to do with Saddam Hussein or any weapons of mass destruction. Invasion of Iraq was on the cards, and Saddam is the excuse. The report says that "even should Saddam pass from the scene," bases in Saudi Arabia and Kuwait would remain permanently as "Iran may well prove as large a threat to U.S. interests as Iraq has."

- The United States should be able to "fight and decisively win multiple, simultaneous major theatre wars," and increase military spending by $48 billion to ensure this.

- The United States should develop "bunker-buster" nuclear weapons. Whereas till now nuclear weapons were considered strategic weapons—a threat of massive retaliation to deter an attack—the development of such uses for smaller nuclear weapons would make them into tactical weapons, that could be used in the ordinary course of battle, as it were. The United States, the report unmistakably implies, should also develop biological weapons: "New methods of attack—electronic, 'non lethal,' biological—will be more widely available.... Combat likely will take place in new dimensions, in space, cyberspace and perhaps the world of microbes.... Advanced forms of biological warfare that can 'target' specific genotypes (i.e., kill people selectively based on their race or ethnicity) may transform biological warfare from the realm of terror to a politically useful tool."

- The United States should create "U.S. Space Forces" to dominate space. The "star wars" program, officially known as National Missile Defense, should be made a priority.

- The report says that "it is time to increase the presence of American forces in Southeast Asia." This may lead to "American and allied power providing the spur to the process of democratization in China." In other words, the United States should strive to replace the present Chinese regime with a clearly pro-American one.

- Supposedly in order to check regimes such as North Korea, Libya, Syria, and Iran the United States military should set up a "worldwide command-and-control system."

- The PNAC supports a "blueprint for maintaining global U.S. preeminence, *precluding the rise of a great power rival,* and shaping the international security order in line with American principles and interests" (emphasis added). Thus the document explicitly calls for preventing the "American century" becoming anyone else's, even if peacefully. Indeed this is the crux of the matter, as we shall see. Close allies such as the U.K. are referred to as "the most effective and efficient means of exercising American global leadership"—that is, a mere mask for American hegemony. Peace keeping missions are described as "demanding American political leadership rather than that of the United Nations."[1]

However, for unleashing this global offensive, what was required was "some catastrophic and catalyzing event—like a new Pearl Harbor" (the U.S. base in Hawaii Japan attacked in 1941, providing the occasion for American entry into World War II).

That event, of course, came with September 11, 2001, accelerating the various missions already charted by the PNAC. As John Pilger points out, the increase in military spending called for by the PNAC has occurred; the development of "bunker-buster" nuclear weapons and "star wars" is taking place; and Iraq is being targeted for the purpose of installing American troops in the Gulf.[2] Further, U.S. forces in Southeast Asia are being beefed up, and North Korea and Iran have been bracketed with Iraq in what George Bush terms an "axis of evil." One should reasonably expect the rest of the PNAC document to be similarly implemented.

It is now clear that the United States intends its invasion of Iraq as only the opening salvo in its invasion of the entire region. This is being made known through semi-official channels, to prepare the ground for future actions. "The road to the entire Middle East goes through Baghdad," said a U.S. administration official to the *Washington Post.* "Once you have a democratic [read "pro-American"] regime in Iraq, like the ones we helped establish in Germany and Japan after World War II, there are a lot of possibilities."[3] In the words of Tariq Aziz, the Iraqi vice president, what the United States wants is not "regime change" but "region change."

Targeting Saudi Arabia

Perhaps the most startling element of this plan is the targeting of Saudi Arabia, long considered the most faithful American ally among the Arab countries—the base for the American assault on Iraq in 1991, a continuing U.S. military base thereafter, the United States' largest market for weapons, the largest supplier of oil to the United States (at a special discount to boot), and the source of up to $600 billion of investments in the United States. On 10 July 2002 a researcher from the RAND Corporation (a prominent think tank created by the U.S. Air Force but now quasi-independent, which regularly does projects for the American defense and foreign policy establishments) made a presentation to the Defense Policy Board—headed, as mentioned earlier, by Perle. The briefing, titled "Taking Saudi out of Arabia,"claimed that "the Arab world has been in a systemic crisis for the last 200 years" and that "since independence, wars have been the principal output of the Arab world." It went on to describe Saudi Arabia in bizarre terms as an enemy of the United States ("the kernel of evil, the prime mover, the most dangerous opponent"; "The Saudis are active at every level of the terror chain, from planners to financiers, from cadre to foot soldier, from ideologist to cheerleader") and recommended that the United States give it an ultimatum to prevent any anti-U.S. activity in Arabia, failing which its oil fields could be seized by U.S. troops and the House of Saud replaced by the Hashemite monarchy that now rules Jordan. The following excerpt gives an idea of the line of thought, if it can be called that:

"Saudi Arabia" is not a God-given entity:

- The House of Saud was given dominion over Arabia in 1922 by the British

- It wrested the Guardianship of the Holy Places—Mecca and Medina—from the Hashemite dynasty

- There is an "Arabia," but it need not be "Saudi"

An ultimatum to the House of Saud:

- Stop any funding and support for any fundamentalist madrasa, mosque, ulama, predicator anywhere in the world

- Stop all anti-U.S., anti-Israeli, anti-Western predication, writings, etc., within Arabia

- Dismantle, ban all of the kingdom's "Islamic charities," confiscate their assets

- Prosecute or isolate those involved in the terror chain, including in the Saudi intelligence services

Or else ...

- What the House of Saud holds dear can be targeted:
  - Oil: the old fields are defended by U.S. forces, and located in a mostly Shiite area

  - Money: the kingdom is in dire financial straits, its valuable assets invested in dollars, largely in the United States

  - The Holy Places: let it be known that alternatives are being canvassed

Other Arabs?:

- The Saudis are hated throughout the Arab world: lazy, overbearing, dishonest, corrupt

- If truly moderate regimes arise, the Wahhabi-Saudi nexus is pushed back into its extremist corner

- The Hashemites have greater legitimacy as Guardians of Mecca and Medina.[4]

The presentation also claimed that the regime change in Iraq would help put pressure on Saudi Arabia, since a major increase in Iraqi oil production would take away the Saudi markets in the West. With reduced dependence on Saudi oil, the United States could confront the House of Saud for (what this presentation alleges to be) its support of terrorism.

While the RAND researcher's aphoristic opus might be dismissed as the work of a fantasist, and the Pentagon did take care immediately to deny that it reflected its views, there are indications that much of it is indeed U.S. policy.

In line with the RAND presentation, Dick Cheney told the national convention of Veterans of Foreign Wars in August that the overthrow of

Saddam would "bring about a number of benefits to the region": "When the gravest of threats are eliminated, the freedom-loving peoples of the region will have a chance to promote the values that can bring lasting peace." According to Patrick Clawson, deputy director of the Washington Institute for Near East Policy, after establishing a pro-U.S. Iraq, "We would be much more in a position of strength vis-à-vis the Saudis." "Everyone will flip out, starting with the Saudis," says Meyrav Wurmser, director of the Center for Middle East Policy at the Hudson Institute in Washington, where Perle is a member of the board. "It will send shock waves throughout the Arab world."[5]

At the behest of a joint congressional committee, the Federal Bureau of Investigation (FBI) has been investigating money transfers from the Saudi ambassador's wife to a Saudi who was friendly with the September 11 hijackers. A $3 trillion lawsuit has been filed in an American court accusing several Saudi institutions and charities and three members of the royal family, including the defense minister, of financing terrorism. Following the filing of this lawsuit, Saudi investors have withdrawn up to $200 billion from the United States.[6]

The United States as Agent Provocateur

Leading political circles in the West are well aware of the United States game plan. Mo Mowlam, a member of Tony Blair's cabinet from 1997-2001, lifted the curtain in an article bluntly titled: "The real goal is the seizure of Saudi oil. Iraq is no threat. Bush wants war to keep U.S. control of the region." She describes how the United States plans to spread the war beyond Iraq:

> What is most chilling is that the hawks in the Bush administration must know the risks involved. They must be aware of the anti-American feeling throughout the Middle East. They must be aware of the fear in Egypt and Saudi Arabia that a war against Iraq could unleash revolutions, disposing of pro-Western governments, and replacing them with populist anti-American Islamist fundamentalist regimes. We should all remember the Islamist revolution in Iran.

The Shah was backed by the Americans, but he couldn't stand against the will of the people. And it is because I am sure that they fully understand the consequences of their actions that *I am most afraid. I am drawn to the conclusion that they must want to create such mayhem* ....

The Americans know they cannot stop such a revolution. They must therefore hope that they can control the Saudi oil fields, if not the government. And what better way to do that than to have a large military force in the field at the time of such disruption. In the name of saving the West, these vital assets could be seized and controlled.... If there is chaos in the region, the United States armed forces could be seen as a global savior. Under cover of the war on terrorism, the war to secure oil supplies could be waged.[7]

A sober gathering of eminent academics, historians, economists, global strategists, and other experts came to a similar consensus at the Oxford Analytica conference in September 2002. The conference predicted that with the invasion of Iraq,

at the very least, violent anti-American street demonstrations in Cairo, Alexandria and other Egyptian cities could be expected—perhaps erupting also in Saudi Arabia and maybe Jordan. These would be forcibly suppressed, but *if they should threaten a number of Middle East regimes, this might not necessarily be outside of the United States game plan,* some experts suggested.... To clean out such regimes and install others that are not just friendly to the United States in foreign policy terms but which also subscribe to American mores would further the cause of the Bush administration's neo-imperialism and also secure the future integrity of energy supplies for the U.S. Such aims might be achieved as part of the greater Iraq campaign—protracted and expensive though this might prove to be—or by using Iraq as a jumping-off point for future regime-destabilizing actions once Saddam Hussein has been subdued.[8]

Israel to Play Key Role

Apparently Israel is accorded a key role in U.S. plans for occupying and policing the region.

According to the leading Israeli historian Martin van Creveld, Israeli prime minister Ariel Sharon's plan is to forcibly "transfer" the two million Palestinians living in the occupied territories to neighboring Jordan—a move opinion polls indicate has the support of 44 percent of Israelis. No doubt this would spark a response from Egypt, Jordan, Syria, and Lebanon (popular sentiment in those regions would irresistibly force the hands of the regimes), but that would merely provide an occasion for Israel to employ once more its overwhelming (American-built and American-funded) military might on them and crush their armies:

> Mr. Sharon would have to wait for a suitable opportunity—such as an American offensive against Iraq.... An uprising in Jordan, followed by the collapse of King Abdullah's regime, would also present such an opportunity—as would a spectacular act of terrorism inside Israel that killed hundreds.
>
> Should such circumstances arise, then Israel would mobilize with lightning speed—even now, much of its male population is on standby. First, the country's three ultra-modern submarines would take up firing positions out at sea. Borders would be closed, a news blackout imposed, and all foreign journalists rounded up and confined to a hotel as guests of the Government. A force of 12 divisions, 11 of them armored, plus various territorial units suitable for occupation duties, would be deployed: five against Egypt, three against Syria, and one opposite Lebanon. This would leave three to face east as well as enough forces to put a tank inside every Arab-Israeli village just in case their populations get any funny ideas.
>
> The expulsion of the Palestinians would require only a few brigades. They would not drag people out of their houses but use heavy artillery to drive them out; the damage caused to Jenin would look like a pinprick in comparison.

Any outside intervention would be held off by the Israeli air force. In 1982, the last time it engaged in large-scale operations, it destroyed 19 Syrian anti-aircraft batteries and shot down 100 Syrian aircraft against the loss of one. Its advantage is much greater now than it was then and would present an awesome threat to any Syrian armored attack on the Golan Heights. As for the Egyptians, they are separated from Israel by 150 miles or so of open desert. Judging by what happened in 1967, should they try to cross it they would be destroyed.

The Jordanian and Lebanese armed forces are too small to count and Iraq is in no position to intervene, given that it has not recovered its pre-1991 strength and is being held down by the Americans.... Some believe that the international community will not permit such an ethnic cleansing. I would not count on it. If Mr. Sharon decides to go ahead, the only country that can stop him is the United States. The U.S., however, regards itself as being at war with parts of the Muslim world that have supported Osama bin Laden. America will not necessarily object to that world being taught a lesson—particularly if it could be as swift and brutal as the 1967 campaign; and also particularly if it does not disrupt the flow of oil for too long.

Israeli military experts estimate that such a war could be over in just eight days. If the Arab states do not intervene, it will end with the Palestinians expelled and Jordan in ruins. If they do intervene, the result will be the same, with the main Arab armies destroyed.[9]

Israel's attack on the Palestinians and then the Arab states would thus complement the United States invasion of Iraq and some other state(s). Israel would hold military sway in the region as the local enforcer of American power.

This explains the unstinted support Sharon has received from Bush for his assault on the Palestinians. The day after his December 3, 2001, meeting with Bush, Sharon besieged Arafat in Ramalla and began the bombing and bombardment of the West Bank. Since then Sharon has not only unleashed death and terror in the occupied territories, but deliberately attempted to humiliate Arafat and discredit him even further among the Palestinians. The attack on Arafat has two objectives: first, to discredit Israel's only existing negotiating party, and thus eliminate the obstacle of negotiations altogether; second, to provoke a reaction from the Palestinians such as can be the excuse for their mass eviction from the occupied territories, just as they were driven out in 1948 from the land that now constitutes Israel. (Van Creveld points out that Sharon has always referred to Jordan as a Palestinian state, the obvious implication being that Palestinians in the occupied territories belong there.)

This entire scenario is perhaps what Cheney had in mind when he said, in his address to the Veterans of Foreign Wars, that the overthrow of Saddam Hussein *would enhance U.S. ability to advance the Israeli-Palestinian peace process.*

Colonial-Style Carve-Up

One analyst rightly compares American plans to the carving-up of the region by Britain and France in the Sykes–Picot treaty of 1916. He lists "Possible scenarios under review at the highest levels":[10]

> Iraq is to be placed under U.S. military rule. Iraq's leadership, notably Saddam Hussein and [Tariq] Aziz, will face U.S. drumhead courts-martial and firing squads.[11]
>
> The swift, ruthless crushing of Iraq is expected to terrify [other] Arab states, Palestinians and Iran into obeying U.S. political dictates.
>
> Independent-minded Syria will be ordered to cease support for Lebanon's Hezbollah, and allow Israel to dominate Jordan and Lebanon, or face invasion and "regime change." The U.S. will anyway undermine the ruling Ba'ath regime and its young leader, Bashir Assad, replacing him with a French-based exile regime. France will get renewed influence in Syria as a consolation prize for losing out in Iraq to the Americans and Brits....
>
> Iran will be severely pressured to dismantle its nuclear and missile programs or face attack by U.S. forces. Israel's rightist Likud party, which guides much of the Bush administration's Mideast thinking, sees Iran, not demolished Iraq, as its principal foe and threat, and is pressing

Washington to attack Iran once Iraq is finished off. At minimum, the U.S. will encourage an uprising against Iran's Islamic regime, replacing it with either a royalist government or one drawn from U.S.-based Iranian exiles.[12]

Saudi Arabia will be allowed to keep the royal family in power, but compelled to become more responsive to U.S. demands and to clamp down on its increasingly anti-American population. If this fails, the CIA is reportedly cultivating senior Saudi air force officers who could overthrow the royal family and bring in a compliant military regime like that of Gen. Pervez Musharraf in Pakistan. Or, partition Saudi Arabia, making the oil-rich eastern portion an American protectorate.

And so on, with Libya's Qaddafi "marked for extinction once bigger game is bagged."

While the apparent targets of the United States assault are the *regimes* of these countries, that would hardly make sense, since none of them poses a threat to the United States, and in fact some of them, such as Saudi Arabia and Egypt, are its client states. Rather the real targets are the anti-imperialist masses of the region, whom certain regimes are unwilling, and others are unable, to control. It is these anti-imperialist masses of West Asia, not their rulers of whatever hue, who have always constituted the real threat to U.S. domination. The United States appears to believe that its overwhelming and highly sophisticated military might can tackle the masses effectively if they come out into the open. That is why it even contemplates *provoking* mass uprisings so as to have occasion to crush them.

Global Hegemonic Drive Parading as National Security

The articles cited above are speculations based on informed official sources; whereas the "National Security Strategy of the United States of America" (released on September 17, 2002; hereafter NSSUSA) is an official statement. It is a remarkable and important document, which deserves a lengthy exposition. (All emphases in the quotations below have been added.)

The twentieth century has yielded a "single sustainable model for national success: freedom, democracy, and free enterprise,"values to be protected "across the globe and across the ages." The United States "enjoys a position of unparalleled military strength and great economic and political influence." "Today, the world's great powers find ourselves on the same side"—that is, the United States lacks any rival. This is "a time of opportunity for America.... The United States will use this moment of opportunity to extend the benefits of freedom across the globe. We will actively work to bring the hope of democracy, development, free markets and free trade to every corner of the world." Thus the "national security" document lays out American *foreign policy.*

Despite its unrivaled supremacy, the United States is faced by a new type of enemy: "shadowy networks of individuals... organized to penetrate open societies.... To defeat this threat we must make use of every tool in our arsenal.... The war against terrorists of global reach is a global enterprise of *uncertain duration. ...*"

Thus the formulation of "terrorism" has solved the problem posed by the present U.S. secretary of state Colin Powell in 1991, when he was chief of U.S. armed forces. "Think hard about it," he said. "I'm running out of demons. I'm running out of villains."[13] In the 1990s, as the United States hunted for the required demon, military spending was slashed and questions were raised about the need for foreign deployments. Condoleezza Rice, the present national security adviser, began a *Foreign Affairs* article in 2000 thus: "The United States has found it exceedingly difficult to define its 'national interest' in the absence of Soviet power." Nicholas Lemann asked her in 2002 whether that was still the case:

"I think the difficulty has passed in defining a role," she said immediately. "I think September 11th was one of those great earthquakes that clarify and sharpen. Events are in much sharper relief." Like Bush, she said that opposing terrorism and preventing the accumulation of weapons of mass destruction "in the hands of irresponsible states" now define the national interest.... Rice said that she had called together the senior staff people of the National Security Council and asked them to think seriously about "*how do you capitalize on these opportunities*" to fundamentally change American doctrine, and the shape of the world, in the wake of September 11th.[14]

In other words, the target is not terrorism. The supposed suppression of terrorism worldwide merely offers "opportunities" for the United States to pursue its strategic agenda without geographic or temporal limits.

NSSUSA finds the mere existence of "terrorists" on a country's soil sufficient justification for the United States to attack the country: "America will hold to account nations that are compromised by terror, including those who harbor terrorists.... We make no distinction between terrorists and those who knowingly harbor or provide aid to them." The phrase "compromised by terror" is vague enough to include those the United States claims have not taken adequately energetic measures against terrorism.

No doubt international law only recognizes the right to self-defense in the face of *imminent attack*, but does not meet the requirements of the United States, which wishes to "adapt the concept of imminent threat" to mean that "America will act against such emerging threats *before they are fully formed*." The mere potential to constitute a "threat" would invite American action. In "identifying and destroying the threat before it reaches our borders ... *we will not hesitate to act alone*," disregarding international forums such as the United Nations.

Global Span
Casting its eye about the world, NSSUSA spells out America's tasks in different regions.

Europe is to be kept subordinate to, and dependent on, American power. For the last decade, the United States has been troubled by the fact that the rationale for the North Atlantic Treaty Organization (NATO), namely the threat from the Soviet bloc, no longer exists. Though Europe is now contemplating setting up its independent military organization, the United States will work "to ensure that these developments work with NATO." The document reshapes NATO as a *global* interventionist force under American leadership: "The alliance must be able to act *wherever our interests are threatened*, creating coalitions under NATO's own mandate, as well as contributing to mission-based coalitions." Rather than develop its own arms industry and forces, Europe should "take advantage of technological opportunities and economies of scale in our defense spending." This is in line with the view of the secret "Defense Planning Guidance," prepared in May 1990 by Paul Wolfowitz and I. Lewis Libby for then defense secretary Dick Cheney and partially leaked to the *New York Times* in the spring of 1992. Mapping out U.S. policy in the wake of the collapse of the Soviet empire, it asserted that "it is of fundamental importance to preserve NATO as the primary instrument of Western defense and security, as well as the channel for U.S. influence and participation in European security affairs. While the United States supports the goal of European integration, *we must seek to prevent the emergence of European-only security arrangements* which would undermine NATO, particularly the alliance's integrated command structures."

NSSUSA issues a blunt warning to China against "pursuing advanced military capabilities that can threaten its neighbors in the Asia-Pacific region." The United States threatens China with interference in its internal affairs: "To make that nation truly accountable to its citizens' needs and aspirations... much work remains to be done." U.S. deployments in the region are to be beefed up, and in order to ensure that American troops are stationed as close as possible to China, South Korea is to be convinced to "maintain vigilance [i.e. hostility] toward the North while preparing our alliance to make contributions to the broader stability of the region over the longer term."

In contrast with China, India is presented as a pillar of American influence in Asia: "We [the United States and India] are the two largest democracies, committed to political freedom protected by representative government. India is moving toward greater economic freedom as well. We have a common interest in the free flow of commerce, including through the vital sea lanes of the Indian Ocean. Finally, we share an interest in fighting terrorism and *in creating a strategically stable Asia.*" Two years ago, India's nuclear rivalry with Pakistan and the battle over Kashmir made it the "most dangerous place on earth" for the United States; now there is not even a single reference to Pakistan or Kashmir, and even India's nuclear and missile programs are treated as "past" concerns. Rather, India is presented as "a growing world power with which we have common strategic interests." (The mere fact of being bracketed with China and Russia as a "potential great power" is deeply satisfying to the Indian ruling elite, which has been angling for some such certificate from the United States—however far from objective reality.)

Preventing the Emergence of Imperialist Rivals

Just as NSSUSA celebrates the United States' unprecedented—and unequaled —strength and influence" as "a time of opportunity," it warns too that it will defend this solitary position. Indeed American *"national security" lies in the absence of any other great power.* "We are attentive to the possible renewal of old patterns of great power competition.... Our military must... dissuade future military competition.... Our forces will be strong enough to dissuade potential adversaries from pursuing a military build-up in hopes of surpassing, or equaling, the power of the United States." This unmistakably echoes the 1990 Defense Planning Guidance document: "Our first objective is to prevent the re-emergence of a new rival, either on the territory of the former Soviet Union or elsewhere, that poses a threat on the order of that posed by the Soviet Union, which requires preventing any hostile power from dominating a region whose resources would, under consolidated control, be sufficient to generate global power. These regions are western Europe, East Asia, the territory of the former Soviet Union, and South west Asia [i.e., the oil-producing region].... Finally, we must maintain the mechanisms for *deterring potential competitors from ever aspiring to a larger regional or global role"* (emphasis added). But whereas the 1990 Defense Planning Guidance was a secret document, the 2002 NSSUSA is a public declaration that the world's sole superpower will not tolerate even potential rivalry.

Massive Expansion of Foreign Deployments

As the mission has no defined enemy, but rather a number of potential rivals to be "dissuaded" from acquiring great power status, it requires a *massive military commitment worldwide.* "To contend with uncertainty and to meet the many security challenges we face, the United States will require bases and stations within and beyond Western Europe and Northeast Asia, as well temporary access arrangements for the long-distance deployment of U.S. forces. Before the war in Afghanistan, that area was low on the list of major planning contingencies. Yet, in a very short time, we had to operate across the length and breadth of that remote nation, using every branch of the armed forces. We must prepare for more such deployments...."

Even outer space is to be brought under U.S. sway: "military capabilities must also...protect critical infrastructure in outer space."

Economic Agenda Merged with Strategic Agenda

It is not merely the threat of violence, or the "emerging," as yet not "fully formed" threat of violence, that constitutes a threat to American national security. "*Free markets and free trade are key priorities of our national security strategy.*" "*Respect for private property*" is among the "*non-negotiable demands of human dignity.*" The economic policies of other countries—their legal and regulatory policies, tax policies ("particularly lower marginal tax rates"), financial systems, fiscal policies, and (what the United States calls) "free trade" are considered part of the "national security" of the United States. "Free trade" is indeed "a moral principle." However, "free trade" refers to *others* opening their markets to the United States. For the United States, NSSUSA prescribes instead "safeguards (that) help ensure that the benefits of free trade do not come at the expense of American workers"—read "American corporations."

Supposedly multilateral institutions, long under the American thumb, are made now explicit instruments of American "national security." The United States will "work with the IMF to streamline the policy conditions for its lending" and "[i]mprove the effectiveness of the World Bank." It will insist that its development assistance is tied to "measurable goals and concrete benchmarks." Countries' development is to be predicated to openness to inflows (and outflows) of capital, and indeed the very objective is merely such openness: "Our long-term objective should be a world in which all countries have investment-grade credit ratings that allow them access to international capital markets and to invest in their future."[15]

Direct Monitoring of "Governance"

A significant aspect of the NSSUSA doctrine is that the United States will now more directly than ever before intervene in and supervise all aspects of "governance" of the lands under its sway. Traditionally, the United States kept its client states' military and foreign policy stance in line, and multiple forces—the IMF, World Bank, bilateral aid, direct pressure from American corporations—kept their economic policies in line. Their widely varying political, social,and cultural institutions were left alone. However, the NSSUSA repeatedly stresses "opening societies and building the infrastructure of democracy," making "freedom and development of democratic institutions key themes in our bilateral relations."

Lest it be imagined, contrary to the experience of a century, that the United States has some fondness for democratic institutions in its client states, it should be noted that these institutions are to be built and run under close American direction—particularly in regard to the means of coercion: "Once the regional campaign [against "terrorism"] localizes the threat to a particular state, we will help ensure the state has the military, law enforcement, political, and financial tools necessary to finish the task." If the outcome of a democratic exercise (such as any one of the elections and referendums won by Hugo Chavez in Venezuela) is not to America's liking, that country will remain targeted and under siege till the people there "reform": "The United States, the international donor community, and the World Bank stand ready to work with a *reformed* Palestinian government [i.e., after the scrapping of the present one] on economic development, increased humanitarian assistance, and a *program to establish, finance, and monitor* a truly independent judiciary."

If a judiciary established by the Americans, paid for by the Americans, and monitored by the Americans can be considered a democratic institution, colonialism is a democratic institution. Indeed, American diplomats are now to be reoriented as viceroys, adept in all matters of governing client states: "Officials trained mainly in international politics must also extend their reach to understand complex issues of domestic governance around the world, including public health, education, law enforcement, the judiciary, and public diplomacy."

The document's repeated mention of education is not an accident: the educational system is one of the media through which the United States is to "wage a war of ideas," carrying out propaganda in its own favor while enforcing the shutting down of schools which propagate anti-American sentiments (while the immediate target is the *madrassas*, the broader target is any democratic anti-imperialist elements in any educational system).

Muslim countries are a special target of this mission: the United States will support "moderate and modern government, especially in the Muslim world, to ensure that the conditions and ideologies that promote terrorism do not find fertile ground in any nation." The United States plans to reform Islam, strengthening the "moderates" in "a clash inside a civilization, a battle for the future of the Muslim world. This is a struggle of ideas and this is an area where America must excel."

The real reason for targeting the Muslim states, of course, has nothing to do with terrorism and everything to do with the fact that, by remarkable coincidence, so many of them—in West Asia, North Africa, the Caspian region, and even Southeast Asia—happen to be rich in hydrocarbons. In that regard, however, the tactful NSSUSA is *Hamlet* without the prince of Denmark: the words "oil," "petroleum," and "hydrocarbons" nowhere occur, and there is just a single reference to working "to expand the sources and types of global energy supplied, especially in the Western Hemisphere, Africa, Central Asia, and the Caspian region."

"Every Weapon"

Finally, the NSSUSA says that "we must make use of every tool in our arsenal," echoing Bush's words after the September 11 attacks: "We will use every necessary weapon of war." It is worth examining the array of weapons the Bush administration plans to use.

Using weapons of mass destruction: There is *active preparation for the use of nuclear weapons.* The March 2002 leak of the Pentagon's "nuclear posture review" revealed that the earlier concept that nuclear weapons are only a form of deterrence, to be used in retaliation against other nuclear powers, has been dumped. The new position foresees the use of "low-yield" nuclear weapons in three scenarios: against targets able to withstand attacks by non-nuclear weapons (such as underground bunkers); in retaliation for an attack with nuclear, biological, or chemical weapons; and *"in the event of surprising military developments,"* such as an "Iraqi attack on Israel or its neighbors, or a North Korean attack on South Korea or a military confrontation over the status of Taiwan." "North Korea, Iraq, Iran, Syria, and Libya are among the countries that could be involved in immediate, potential or unexpected contingencies," it says.

A report published last year by America's National Institute for Public Policy, a right-wing think tank, declared that "nuclear weapons can ... be used in counter-force attacks that are intended to neutralize enemy military capabilities." The authors of the report include senior Pentagon officials and the deputy national security adviser. Geoff Hoon, British defense secretary, told MPs earlier this year: "I am absolutely confident, in the right conditions, we would be willing to use our nuclear weapons."[16]

The talk of "low-yield" nuclear weapons is merely to prepare the ground for using nuclear weapons as such. The Defense Threat Reduction Agency, a $1.1 billion agency set up in 1998, is studying how to attack hardened and deeply buried bunkers with high-yield nuclear weapons.[17]

The price in human lives would be terrible. According to the Washington-based Physicians for Social Responsibility (PSR), a "mini-nuke" attack on Saddam Hussein's presidential bunker would cause 20,000 deaths in Baghdad. Many more would be maimed, burned, and suffer the effects of radiation. No cause for concern, believe the Americans: while a careful study by Jonathan Steele in the *Guardian*, drawing on a variety of sources including estimates by aid agencies, reveals over 20,000 Afghans died as a result of the United States invasion, there is hardly a mention of the fact in the world press outside of his article.[18] Nor is there coverage of the study by the Medical Association for the Prevention of War, Australia, which estimates that *a U.S. attack on Iraq would cost between 48,000 and 260,000 lives immediately and 200,000 from the effects of the war.* The study, whose methodology has been endorsed by the former chief of the Australian Defense Forces, also says that the use of nuclear weapons would raise the toll to millions.

Until now *biological weapons programs* have been carried on under cover of peaceful uses. Now the Pentagon is openly pushing for the development of offensive biological weapons "to produce systems that will degrade the warfighting capabilities of potential adversaries."While leading naval and air force laboratories presented proposals to this effect in 1997, the Marine Corps has now submitted them for assessment by the United States National Academy of Sciences.[19] The NSSUSA's eagerness to get control of the public health systems of third world countries should be seen in this light.

Agent provocateurs, disinformation: A secret army has been set up by the Pentagon. It will unite CIA and military covert action, information warfare, and deception. ("Information warfare" is the deliberate spread of falsehoods as a weapon of war.) Its purpose would be to provoke terrorist attacks which would then justify "counter attack" by the United States on countries "harboring the terrorists":

> Rumsfeld's influential Defense Science Board 2002 Summer Study on Special Operations and Joint Forces in Support of Countering Terrorism says in its classified "outbrief"—a briefing drafted to guide other Pentagon agencies—that the global war on terrorism "requires new strategies, postures and organization." The board recommends creation of a super-Intelligence Support Activity, an organization it dubs the Proactive, Preemptive Operations Group (P2OG), to bring together CIA and military covert action, information warfare, intelligence, and cover and deception. Among other things, this body would launch secret operations aimed at *"stimulating reactions"* among ter-

rorists and states possessing weapons of mass destruction—that is, for instance, prodding terrorist cells into action and exposing themselves to "quick-response" attacks by U.S. forces. Such tactics would hold "states/sub-state actors accountable" and "signal to harboring states that their sovereignty will be at risk," the briefing paper declares.[20]

The *New York Times* reported in February 2002 that the Pentagon's new "Office of Strategic Influence" (OSI) is "developing plans to provide news items, possibly even false ones, to foreign media organizations" in an effort "to influence public sentiment and policy makers in both friendly and unfriendly countries." The OSI was created shortly after September 11, 2001, supposedly to publicize the U.S. government's perspective in Islamic countries and to generate support for the United States' "war on terror." According to the *Times*, "one of the military units assigned to carry out the policies of the Office of Strategic Influence" is the U.S. Army's Psychological Operations Command (PSYOPS).[21]

Although public outrage caused the OSI to be officially scrapped, a contemptuous remark by Rumsfeld on 18 November 2002 reveals that only the name has been scrapped:

> "And then there was the Office of Strategic Influence. You may recall that. And 'oh my goodness gracious isn't that terrible, Henny Penny the sky is going to fall.' I went down that next day and said fine, if you want to savage this thing fine I'll give you the corpse. There's the name. You can have the name, but I'm gonna keep doing every single thing that needs to be done and I have."[22]

According to William Arkin, Rumsfeld is redesigning the U.S. military to make "information warfare" central to its functions. This new policy, says Arkin, increasingly "blurs or even erases the boundaries between factual information and news, on the one hand, and public relations, propaganda, and psychological warfare, on the other."[23]

The scale of war crimes in the offing is indicated by the Bush administration's eagerness to get immunity from such charges. It has despatched senior diplomats to Europe to insist that governments of the European Union grant blanket immunity to all U.S. citizens from the United Nations' newly formed International Criminal Court, which is to try cases of genocide, war crimes and other human rights abuses.[24] Although the likelihood of any American being hauled up before a UN body is very slim, the Bush administration is taking no chances.

Clearly, current U.S. plans represent a radical break from traditional strategies for maintaining global domination. This sudden consensus among all sectors of the United States ruling class for bold and potentially risky action can only be understood as a response to a profoundly threatening economic crisis.

HOME FRONT IN SHAMBLES

Even as the United States prepares to launch an invasion of Iraq (and perhaps of other countries as well), its economy is trapped in a recession with no clear prospect of recovery. True to their character, the world's giant media corporations have not seen fit to explore the causal connection between these two outstanding facts.

No doubt the recession has been extraordinarily mild by historical standards—in fact, going by the narrow official definition and available data, the U.S. economy is now out of the recession, and has begun to grow again. However, this upturn is illusory: all signs point to the United States returning to recession soon, if indeed it has not done so already. Moreover, the official definition of "recession" is itself dubious—for instance, there has been no real pick up in employment during the so-called recovery. The U.S. corporate sector knows the truth: corporate profits and business investment have experienced their steepest decline since the 1930s.

Importantly, the United States is not alone in its fate: Japan has been stuck in recession for a decade, and Europe has now joined the club. Whereas, in the recent past, buoyant U.S. demand was the motor pulling the world economy out of recession, today the United States itself is in the doldrums and no other economy is taking its place as the demand motor. Prospects for a global recovery are bleak. Indeed, the giant overhang of debt and excess capacity dictates that the recession must deepen.

Three years ago, economic analysts and the financial press were still celebrating the American economy's seemingly endless capacity for growth. Alan Greenspan, the head of the U.S. Federal Reserve (the American central bank), was treated as a media star for his genius in fine-tuning interest rates to avoid both inflation and recession. Some advanced the novel theory that new technology, continuous productivity growth, and globalization had made the American economy recession-proof.

Crisis of Overproduction in Full Bloom

It is in times of economic setback that the press returns to earth. The Chicago Tribune recently published a series of articles on the current crisis, drawing on a wide range of interviews with employers, employees, and economic analysts. The first piece in the series is titled: "The Economics of Glut. Bloated industries put the economy in a bind. Glut is making it harder to shake off the recession." The article begins: "The world's auto industry can now produce 20 million more cars than consumers can buy." Citing instances also from telecommunications and dot-coms, the Tribune discovers that "economists call the phenomenon overcapacity.... Businesses can produce far more than we need. Supply has simply out-stripped demand. When that happens, production slows, equipment sits idle, costs go up, workers are laid off and investments are postponed. The capacity glut exists on a scale that this country and many others haven't seen for decades, and it at least partially explains why it is so difficult for the American economy to shake off a recession that by all measures seemed mild."

The *Tribune* sees a swamp of excess capacity in airline, auto, machine tool, steel, textile, and high-tech industries, even commercial space and hotel rooms. According to the Federal Reserve, manufacturers are using only 73.5 percent of capacity, far below the 80.9 percent average of 1967-2001, and 3.5 percentage points below the level during the 1990-91 recession. In an effort to attract customers, airlines have slashed their fares to five-year lows; United Airlines, the second largest in the country, has filed for bankruptcy; and Boeing says its deliveries of airplanes will be down 28 percent this year.[25]

The telecommunications industry took on *$2.1 trillion* in debt between 1996 and 2000 and jacked up investment by 15 percent per year in real terms.[26] Each firm tried to steal a march on the others, on the basis of projections of a massive growth in demand. By 2000 the telecom industry accounted for a quarter of the increase in the U.S. economy's equipment spending. Today the world has 39 million miles of fiber optic lines, and telecom networks are operating at *3 percent* of their capacity.

Despite forty-five semiconductor fabricating plants having shut down in the United States, the American semiconductor industry is said to suffer from 15 percent overcapacity. This figure is set to rise: apparently China has built some of the largest advanced semiconductor plants in the world.

The U.S. automobile industry—still the country's most important industry—can produce 2 million more cars than it can sell. The big three manufacturers—General Motors, Ford, and Chrysler—are dealing with the collapse of demand by financing customers at zero percent interest. Sales are projected to fall from 17.5 million last year to 17 million this year and 16.5 million next year. Ford is planning to slash production by 16 percent, or 900,000 vehicles, by 2004, shutting five plants and slashing 12,000 jobs.

Under monopoly capital the build up of overcapacity doesn't immediately result in a cutback in investment. Indeed, firms are driven to invest on an even grander scale, to outspend their rivals and thereby grab market share away from them—a strategy pursued by all the firms, with predictable results. In 1998 the world automobile industry, the largest manufacturing industry, could make 18 million more cars than it could sell, and Japanese car makers were running at 50 percent of their capacity;[27] that gap has risen to 20 million. Automobile giants have been setting up plants in their rivals' countries the better to penetrate their markets.

Investment Now Not Responding to Stimuli

When the authorities conceded in late 2001 that recession had already set in, they ascribed it partly to the September 11 attacks and exuded confidence that it would be brief. The necessary measures were in fact already in motion: Lower interest rates and tax cuts were meant to induce businesses and consumers to spend more, and so boost demand for firms' products and services, in turn giving a fillip to investment. However, despite the passage of a ten-year tax reduction package of $1.35 trillion, and the Federal Reserve's slashing interest rates twelve times over thirteen months, the "recovery" is pallid.

"Even more unsettling," says the *Tribune,* "is the fact that falling prices—or deflation—have taken hold in the manufacturing sector. Prices of goods have been dropping as a global excess capacity has developed. There are some indications that deflation is beginning to spill over into the services sector, in areas like retail trade, which is indirectly related to manufacturing. The U.S. hasn't had a generalized deflation since the Great Depression in the 1930s. In a deflationary environment, people postpone purchases in anticipation that prices could be lower in the future. Demand drops. Profits spiral downward. Jobs are lost. Retrenchment sets in."[28]

Unemployment rose from 3.9 percent in September 2000 to 6 percent in November 2002, and won't fall in foreseeable future. Three million jobs have been slashed—2 million in manufacturing. The vast excess capacity means that even the slight pick up in growth hasn't translated into more jobs. A year ago, there were one million people who had been unemployed 26 weeks or longer; now there are 1.7 million. The retrenchments are particularly large in the "new economy" sectors: Brenner points out that "In the very brief period between the end of 2000 and the middle of 2002, as more than sixty companies went bankrupt, the telecommunications industry laid off more than 500,000 workers, which is 50 percent more than it hired in its spectacular expansion between 1996 and 2000."[29]

Not to worry, says the Federal Reserve. More interest rate reductions are on the way. "But by now," says the *Economist,* "the Fed has shot most of its ammunition: with interest rates and inflation already so low, there is little room for further easing if the economy stumbles. That raises the spectre of falling prices, which would be devastating in an economy so awash with debt"[30]—as the value of assets for which people have borrowed plummet, this sets off a devastating chain of defaults and bankruptcies throughout the economy.

Overcapacity in U.S. industry—and indeed the world—isn't new. It has been a perennial underlying feature of monopoly capital, and so of the American economy. Capacity utilization in U.S. manufacturing has been on a steady downward trend since the sixties.[31] It is huge overcapacities in manufacturing worldwide that explain the *decade*-long recession in Japan—an economy that is at the forefront of manufacturing efficiency.[32] It is again giant global overcapacities in industries such as computer chips that underlay the collapse of the Southeast Asian economies in 1997–1998. The Southeast Asian economies were shortly followed by Russia and Brazil, and then Argentina in 2000. Recession in the United States and Europe is only the latest act in this as yet unfolding drama.

Endemic to Capitalism

How do such overcapacities develop? Capitalists invest in order to earn a profit, and how much they invest, in which industries, using which technologies, and so on are determined by the prospect for profits. In the course of competing with one another to grab market shares and to maximize their profits, capitalists must continuously expand their productive capacity. The purpose of production under capitalism is to accumulate more capital.

However, in this process the growth of productive capacity soon outstrips demand. (Seriously redistributing income throughout society would no doubt increase demand, but it would take away profits from capitalists, going against the very reason for existence of investment under capitalism.) As demand weakens, the profitability of investment declines; capitalists therefore cut back on investment; demand for investment goods suffers, and, as workers get retrenched, demand for consumer goods further weakens. This is how recessions come about.

Capitalist theorists claim that the scrapping of capacity and the depression of wages (due to mass unemployment and the desperation of workers to work at any price) eventually make it profitable for capitalists to invest again. Indeed, these factors may work the other way. Workers may be available more cheaply, but with less money in the hands of workers in general, demand would stay depressed, and the capitalist would be reluctant to invest again. In the absence of some counter acting force *outside* the forces just described, production and employment would remain at a level far below the productive capacity of the economy. The Great Depression persisted through the 1930s despite wages falling dramatically.

Such a crisis is peculiar to capitalism. Under earlier historical social systems, there were no doubt periods when growth—or even production itself—declined. However, the causes were generally natural calamities or war. Unique to capitalism is the strange phenomenon of production falling because of *the ability to produce too much.* The further growth of production is held back not by physical limits to production (equipment, raw materials, labor power) or by physical limits to consumption (even if needs for a particular commodity were completely satisfied, investment could move to fulfilling other needs). Rather, production is held back because it is not *profitable* for the capitalists to produce more.

The only way to resolve this contradiction—establishing the social control of the surplus, so that it is deployed not according to private profit but social need—is by definition impossible under capitalism. Instead, capitalists and their governments employ various methods to deal with the effects of this contradiction. These methods do deal with some effects for some time, without making the contradiction go away—the use of these methods could even accentuate the contradiction when it finally once again surfaces. It is important to grasp that it is not the policy of one or the other administration or country, but this contradiction itself, a necessary part of capitalism, that propels the entire dynamic.

Why then aren't capitalist economies always in crisis? Because they have been able to draw on various counter acting forces outside the process of capital accumulation described above. In the past century, such forces generating demand came from different sources. It was only once the United States entered World War II, and the needs of war created full employment of labor and industrial capacity, that the country really emerged from the Great Depression that began in 1929. After the war, there were the needs of postwar rebuilding, as well as pent-up demand for consumer goods postponed during the war; then demand continued to be boosted by wars in Korea and Vietnam, and the Cold War, requiring massive arms expenditures even in peacetime.

Finally, however, the economy came to rely, for generating demand, more and more on an explosion of debt (consumer, corporate, national), and on a *financial-speculative sector whose growth far outstripped the growth of commodity-producing sectors.*[33]

The Biggest Bubble in America's History

Under capitalism, as we mentioned above, profitability ultimately determines investment, but under monopoly capital the day of reckoning can be put off for some time with the help of state intervention (physical, fiscal, and financial). U.S. corporate profitability, it now emerges, turned dramatically downward in 1997 in the face of worldwide overcapacity. Brenner points out that "Between 1997 and 2000, at the very same time as the much-vaunted U.S. economic expansion was reaching its peak, corporate profits in absolute terms and the rate of return on capital stock (plant, equipment, and software) in the non financial corporate economy were falling sharply—as recently revised figures show, by 15–20 percent in both cases!"[34]

Despite this share prices soared, fueled by cheaper and cheaper funds as the Federal Reserve repeatedly loosened interest rates. What took place was the biggest credit boom in U.S. history. The wealthy, finding the prices of their shares soaring, consumed more. Corporations borrowed and bought back their shares, pushing up their share prices further and thus getting access to cheap funds. With these funds they made massive new investments. No doubt profitability kept plummeting, but unscrupulous auditors were hired to cook the books. Among the 27 *major* corporations so far found guilty of such practices are such stars as AOL Time Warner, Enron, Worldcom, and Xerox. The two top U.S. banks, Citigroup and J. P. Morgan Chase, as well as Merrill Lynch, and the country's top auditing firm, Arthur Andersen, are also deeply implicated.

In the words of the *Economist*,

This is no normal business cycle, but the bursting of the biggest bubble in America's history. Never before have shares become so overvalued. Never before have so many people owned shares. And never before has every part of the economy invested (indeed, overinvested) in a new technology with such gusto. All this makes it likely that the hangover from the binge will last longer and be more widespread than is generally expected....

The most recent bubble was not confined to the stock market: instead, the whole economy became distorted. Firms overborrowed and overinvested on unrealistic expectations about future profits and the belief that the business cycle was dead. Consumers ran up huge debts and saved too little, believing that an ever rising stock market would boost their wealth. The boom became self-reinforcing as rising profit expectations pushed up share prices, which increased investment and consumer spending. Higher investment and a strong dollar helped to hold down inflation and hence interest rates, fueling faster growth and higher share prices.

The outcome has been catastrophic:

Since March 2000 the S&P 500 index [an index of share prices] has fallen by more than 40 percent. *Some $7 trillion has been wiped off the value of American shares, equivalent to two-thirds of annual GDP. And yet share prices still look expensive* [i.e. they will fall more].[35]

Yet to Hit Bottom

We described earlier the theory of business cycles to which the American establishment, including Alan Greenspan, subscribes. According to this theory, overinvestment and high employment finally result in declining profitability, triggering a recession. Through the recession, the earlier "excesses" are purged: capacity is scrapped and workers retrenched. Finally comes a point at which forces accumulate to reverse the downward direction, and it is profitable to invest again. However, by this standard theory the recession should be nowhere near its end, since the *ear-*

lier excesses are not being purged at all. Instead the Federal Reserve's answer to the downturn is to pump in more debt, as the *Economist* notes with concern:

> A good indication of the size of the adjustment yet to be made is the private sector's financial balance (or private-sector net saving, equivalent to saving minus investment).... In the United States the private sector balance shifted from a surplus of 5 percent of GDP in 1992 to a deficit of 5 percent of GDP in 2000 as households and firms went on a borrowing spree, an astonishing change after almost four decades when the private sector never ran a deficit at all....
>
> Troublingly, consumers have continued to borrow as if little has changed. By slashing interest rates, the Fed has encouraged a house-price boom that has partially offset equity losses and allowed households to take out bigger mortgages to prop up their spending.... Households' debt-service payments are ... close to a record high, even though interest rates are low.
>
> Households cannot keep borrowing at their current pace. At some stage they will need to start saving more and spending less. If this happens abruptly, it will trigger another, deeper recession.... America's economy now looks awfully like Japan's in the early 1990s.[36]

Even as American households do borrow massively for consumption, the American manufacturing sector has become increasingly unable to compete with imports. For every dollar of goods it exports, the United States is now spending $1.43 on imports. It is running a monthly trade deficit of more than $40 billion a month, or nearly $500 billion a year. American commentators worry that the American manufacturing base is being whittled away. Smaller American manufacturers are pressing for a substantial devaluation of the dollar to make American goods cheaper than foreign ones, and thus better able to compete. As we shall see below, this solution is ruled out for the United States, since it runs counter to the interests of the United States' global *financial* hegemony.

The Secret to a Limitless Debt: Dollar Hegemony

Normally, a country whose national debt grows rapidly faces serious problems. Investors worry that it will not be able to service its debts, and they begin withdrawing their investments; bankers refuse to provide it fresh loans; and the country soon suffers a balance of payments crisis. If the debtor is a third world country, it is forced to turn for loans to the International Monetary Fund and the World Bank. These two institutions in turn stipulate a program of "structural adjustment," which depresses the consumption of the vast majority, depresses the cost of labor power, cheapens the country's raw materials exports, hawks off public sector assets and natural resources to foreign investors at cut-rate prices, and so on.

However, until now the United States has been able to run up a truly giant national debt for a special reason. Being the world's leading capitalist economy, and a military superpower, its currency has been used for payments between countries (and therefore for their reserves of foreign exchange as well). When it needs to pay its debts it merely issues a Treasury bond (i.e. borrows from the capital market) to which investors from around the world rush to subscribe. Foreign investors buy not only bonds issued by the government but also American corporate bonds, shares, and real estate. These inflows, soaking up as they do the world's savings, ensure that the United States is able to import more than it exports, year after year, without suffering the treatment handed out by the IMF and World Bank to countries like Argentina, Brazil, India, and so on.

This endless supply of golden eggs depends on the United States remaining the supreme imperialist power and the dollar remaining the currency for international payments. However, that is precisely what is now threatened.

The Role of Oil in Dollar Hegemony

During World War II, the Bretton Woods conference worked out post war international financial arrangements with the aim of ensuring the imperialist powers' stability, providing for their growth, and avoiding the types of financial crises witnessed in the preceding decades. Among other things, the conference fixed the value of the U.S. dollar in gold—$35 to an ounce. Holders of U.S. dollars could convert them into gold at their option. This posed no problem as long as no one wanted to do so. But, from the mid-1960s, when inflation (brought on by increased spending on the Vietnam War and welfare programs) reduced the value of the dollar, foreign dollar holders began converting their dollars to gold.

Alarmed at its declining gold supplies, the United States first devalued the dollar relative to gold in 1971 and, in 1973, unilaterally declared it would no longer be convertible into gold. If, despite this severe shock, countries continued to accept the dollar as the currency for international payments and investors continued to put their money in dollars, it was because of America's continuing supremacy worldwide and the absence of a competing international currency. U.S. control over oil producers played a crucial role. Arjun Makhijani notes:

> Oil exporters—led by Iran, Venezuela, and Saudi Arabia—decided to continue denominating the price of oil in U.S. dollars, ostensibly a sign of confidence in the United States and in its money. But, in fact, these countries had little choice but to continue to use U.S. dollars—there was simply no realistic global alternative at the time.
>
> With oil linked to the dollar, and a substantial U.S. military presence in the Middle East, the position of the dollar seemed to be strong. At that time, Iran was the closest U.S. ally in the Persian Gulf and welcomed U.S. military presence. Iran was also the most powerful military force and the most populous country in the region, as well as the world's second largest oil exporter.
>
> To date, the oil-dollar link has given the United States a huge advantage in international trade. Corporations and countries carry out trade in U.S. dollars, making the U.S. Treasury and the U.S. Federal Reserve Board the ultimate arbiters of global monetary policy. However, the stability of the U.S. dollar, and by extension the global monetary system, partially depends on the financial policies of Persian Gulf countries that control nearly two-thirds of the world's reserve of "black gold" [petroleum].

That weakness became evident in 1979, when the Shah of Iran was overthrown by Ayatollah Khomeini's Islamic revolution, and the United States lost its main military ally in the global oil patch. The price of oil shot up to $40 a barrel (about three times today's level in real terms) and the value of the dollar plummeted relative to other currencies. The price of gold soared to $800 per ounce. The U.S. had to drastically increase interest rates—to 15 to 20 percent, causing the most severe recession since World War II—to encourage foreigners to hold on to their U.S. dollars rather than dump them for other currencies.[37]

It is worth summing up the points made above:

- The United States, and indeed the world economy, is suffering from a crisis of overproduction.

- In order to stave off recession, the U.S. Federal Reserve has been boosting demand by pumping in unprecedented amounts of credit.

- The United States has the funds to do this because foreigners put their savings in U.S. dollar assets.

- The United States' overall global supremacy and in particular its control over oil have sustained its status as the safest harbour for international capital.

- However, U.S. ability to soak up the world's savings is a double-edged sword. If foreigners, who hold half or more of all U.S. currency, should decide to dump the dollar, its value would plummet, leading to yet more capital flying from the country.

- In order to prevent that happening, and to get foreign capital to return, the United States would have to raise its interest rates steeply.

- But if that were to be done, given the vast addition to U.S. debt since 1980, this time a steep U.S. interest rate hike could cause a crash heard round the world. This would happen because debt-laden American corporations and consumers would be unable to service their debts, so their assets would flood the market; asset prices would collapse, and banks—swamped with worthless assets instead of income—would in turn collapse. In short, there is a threat of a new Great Depression.

Implications of the Euro

In the 1970s, there was no alternative to the dollar. On January 1, 1999, an alternative arose in the form of the euro, the new currency of the European Union (EU). Of course, investors did not immediately flock to the euro. The euro stuttered at birth, falling 30 percent against the dollar by the end of 2000. In the last year, however, it has picked up sharply, and in recent months has remained at parity with the dollar (i.e., about one euro per dollar).

The euro has become attractive for three reasons:

First, since the EU is a large imperialist economy, about the same size as the United States, it is an attractive and stable investment for foreign investors.

Secondly, since foreign investors' holdings are overwhelmingly in dollars, they wish to diversify and thus reduce the risk of losses in case of a dollar decline: they are increasingly nervous at the size of the U.S. debt mountain and the failure of the U.S. government to tackle this problem.

Thirdly, certain countries smarting under American military domination sense that the rule of the dollar is now vulnerable, and see the switch to the euro as a way to hit back.

Thus even in November 2000, when the euro was 30 percent down against the dollar, Iraq demanded UN approval to be paid in euros in the UN oil-for-food program. This despite the fact that the currency markets at the time did not see a rebound for the euro and despite the fact that Iraq would make the switch at considerable immediate cost, losing 10 cents a barrel to compensate buyers for their currency conversion costs. Iraq also asked that the $10 billion in its frozen bank account in New York be converted to euros. The UN, a plaything of the United States, resisted the change until Iraq threatened to suspend its oil exports.[38]

Iran, which the United States has now labeled, along with Iraq and North Korea, as part of an "axis of evil," is also contemplating switching to the euro. The Iran National Oil Company welcomed the launch of the euro in 1998 itself, stating, "This money will free us from the rule of the dollar," and we "will adopt it." The national oil company and other major Iranian companies have made it clear to both their European and Latin American oil partners that they would "prefer the euro." While Iran continued using the dollar thereafter, there are indications it could follow Iraq's example. The Iranian government budget for the year to March 2002 was tabulated in dollars, but in December 2001 an oil ministry official said that "could change in the future." *Iran News* called for a switch to the euro for both oil and non-oil trade: "The euro could become our currency of choice" if it made gains on the dollar.[39] Since then the euro has climbed 14 percent against the dollar.[40]

Some in Saudi Arabia have called for switching to the euro as "a more effective punishment [than an oil embargo] for the United States, Israel's principal source of financial and political support."[41]

At the Russia-European Union summit in May 2001,

EU leaders... made an audacious bid to lure Russia away from its reliance on the greenback [the dollar], calling on Moscow to start accepting euros instead of dollars for its exports, dangling the attractive carrot of a boom in investment and trade.

In a report commissioned by Russia's Central Bank in July 1999, the Russian Academy of Science said: "The introduction of the euro directly bears on the strategic interests of Russia and alters the conditions for its integration into the world economy. In the final analysis, the consequences are to the benefit of our country." Olga Butorina from the Academy of Science said whereas EU states accounted for 33 percent of trade turnover in 1998 compared with 8 percent for the United States, 80 percent of foreign trade contracts—mainly for oil, gas, and other commodities—were concluded in dollars.... "[Switching to the euro] would increase dramatically the demand for euros in the world," she said. "For sure, it would be an important strategic shift and the euro would start to compete with the dollar in international trade markets."[42]

Another likely candidate for switching to the euro is Venezuela, whose leader Hugo Chavez the United States has been attempting to oust over the last year, without success (at the time of going to press). It is not only the oil economies that would make the switch (for example, North Korea recently said it would convert its foreign exchange reserves to the euro); but the shift of the major oil exporters to accepting payment in euros would indeed have a major, potentially devastating, impact on the dollar.

The more countries that switch to the euro, the more attractive the euro would become.

Dollar Slide Threatens

As the dollar's share of trade declines, central banks will want their foreign exchange reserves to be similarly distributed. Asian central banks have accounted for 80 percent of the growth in global foreign exchange reserves, with current holdings of a gargantuan *$1.5 trillion*, most of it invested in American bonds. Around 85 percent of Asian central bank reserves are estimated to be in U.S. dollars. A shift of just 15 percent would subtract $225 billion from the dollar and add it to the euro.

The revelations that a stellar gallery of American corporations led by Enron and Worldcom have been cooking their books, and that U.S. manufacturing corporations' profits fell by 65 percent between their 1997 peak and 2002[43] would also unnerve foreign investors—who own a reported $1.5 trillion in U.S. corporate equities.[44]

Of course, there are certain checks on these trends. For one, the world's major financial centers are still New York and London, and Britain has still not joined the euro. The euro has as yet no financial center to rival London and New York. Thus Iran is hesitant to actually make the switch to the euro because London is still the financial center for Iran overseas business.

Moreover, neither Europe nor the Asian economies want to see the U.S. economy collapse. First, they would not be able to liquidate their holdings in the United States before that happened, and therefore would suffer huge losses. Secondly, the collapse of the U.S. market for their goods would deal them a heavy blow. Thirdly, if the dollar lost value American goods would become cheap in terms of other currencies, and displace European and Asian goods in their home markets. So, unlike Iraq, the EU and Asia would want to proceed slowly, protecting the value of their investments as they withdrew them.

However, that is assuming rational collective behavior on the part of investors, far removed from reality. Once a sudden shift takes place, herd behavior takes over. As each investor races to pull out his investments, investors collectively drag down the value of all their investments. "We seem to be approaching the cliff edge," says Avinash Persaud, head of research at State Street, a leading New York–based investment bank. "Even if everyone expects just a modest fall in the dollar they end up getting a violent one, simply because everyone will wait before buying" the dollar.[45]

U.S. Unilateralism
During this period, the United States has damaged its chances of cooperative action with Europe and east Asia by going on a rampage of unilateralism. Examples abound:

- It has dismissed the binding obligations of the Kyoto Protocol on Climate Change, and thus thrust the burden of preventing global warming on the rest of the world.

- It has refused to be bound by the newly set-up International Criminal Court.

- It has refused to sign the treaty banning anti-personnel mines.

- It has dumped the process of strengthening the Biological Weapons Convention.

- It has rejected the Comprehensive Test Ban Treaty, which the previous U.S. administration was trying to force third world countries like India to sign, and is preparing to test a fresh generation of nuclear weapons, which it now calmly says it plans to use against non-nuclear countries as well.

- It has unilaterally withdrawn from the Anti Ballistic Missile Treaty and is racing to set up a space-based "shield" against missiles (the National

Missile Defense, which will indeed enable it to strike others with nuclear weapons and not fear reprisal). It thus creates scope to seize control of outer space.

- It has openly threatened the UN that it would be rendered irrelevant if it did not follow American dictates.

After extracting an unprecedented declaration from NATO that the September 11 attack on the United States would be treated as an attack on all NATO member states, the United States ignored NATO for the Afghanistan invasion and assigned European forces only such lowly jobs as policing.

In trade, the United States has leveled heavy tariffs on European steel imports in order to protect its own industry. It has unilaterally retaliated at what it sees as European restrictions on imports of American beef and bananas, each retaliation accounting for a $100 million or so of annual trade, and has rejected all European efforts to resolve these disputes. Without sanction from any international body, the United States levels sanctions against European firms that deal with American enemies such as Cuba and Iran.

More trade clashes loom. The world's biggest airplane makers, the American Boeing and the European Airbus, are fighting a frenzied battle for shrinking orders. In 2003, a dispute is set to explode over agricultural subsidies, genetically modified products, and overall agricultural trade.[46]

In Asia, the threat to the United States could come from the increasing trend toward the setting up of an economic bloc on the lines of the EU. China, Japan, South Korea, and the Southeast Asian countries are moving slowly toward an East Asian free trade area. South Korea, Indonesia, and Thailand have suffered the humiliation of begging for IMF loans during the 1997–1998 crisis. The loans were given on condition that they follow austerity measures that merely suppressed economic activity and made their firms cheap for American corporations to buy up. This experience has spurred the moves to set up cooperative arrangements to prevent currency collapses, and eventually establish an Asian Monetary Fund (AMF) for this purpose. Since these countries have $1.5 trillion of foreign exchange reserves between them, the AMF would rival the U.S.-dominated IMF. These developments may move in the direction of a common currency at some point in the future.[47] The United States is strenuously attempting to prevent the emergence of such a separate bloc. It sees the growing integration of capitalist China with the Southeast Asian economies as an important threat.[48]

As the global recession sets in, with the U.S., Europe, and Japan sinking together, tensions are likely to sharpen between these three blocs. Cooperative effort to boost global demand is less likely than is competition among them to get the biggest share.

MILITARY SOLUTION TO AN ECONOMIC CRISIS

Indeed Washington has taken the contrary course. It plans to reverse the trends mentioned above by seizing *the world's richest oil-producing regions.* This it deems necessary for three related reasons:

1. Securing U.S. supplies: The United States itself is increasingly dependent on oil imports—already a little over half its daily consumption of 20 million barrels is imported. It imports its oil from a variety of sources—Canada, Venezuela, Nigeria, Saudi Arabia, even Iraq. But its own production is falling and will continue to fall steadily even as its consumption continues to grow. In the future, inevitably, it will become increasingly dependent on oil from West Asia–North Africa, a region where the masses of ordinary people despise the United States, where three of the leading oil producers (Iraq, Iran, and Libya) are professedly anti-American, and the others (Saudi Arabia, Kuwait, the United Arab Emirates) are in danger of being toppled by anti-American forces. The United States, of course, is doing its best to tie up or seize supplies from other regions—West Africa, northern Latin America, the Caspian region. And yet the United States cannot escape the simple arithmetic:

The U.S. Department of Energy and the International Energy Agency both project that global oil demand could grow from the current 77 million barrels a day (mbd) to 120 mbd in 20 years, driven by the United States and the emerging markets of south and east Asia. The agencies assume that most of the supply required to meet this demand must come from OPEC, whose production is expected to jump from 28 mbd in 1998 to 60 mbd in 2020. *Virtually all of this increase would come from the Middle East, especially Saudi Arabia.*

A simple fact explains this conclusion: 63 percent of the world's proven oil reserves are in the Middle East, 25 percent (or 261 billion barrels) in Saudi Arabia alone....

Although Asian demand for oil is expected to grow dramatically in coming decades, no other economy rivals that of the United States for the growth of its oil imports. Over the past decade, the increase in the United States' share of the oil market, in terms of trade, was higher than the total oil consumption in any other country, save Japan and China. The United States' increase in imports accounts for more than a third of the total increase in oil trade and more than half of the total increase in OPEC's production during the 1990s. This fact, together with the fall in U.S. oil production, means that the United States will remain the single most important force in the oil market.[49]

Given its growing dependence on oil imports, the United States cannot afford to allow the oil producing regions to be *under the influence of any other power, or independent.*[50]

2. Maintaining dollar hegemony: If other imperialist powers were able to displace U.S. dominance in the region, the dollar would be dealt a severe blow. The pressure for switching to the euro would become irresistible and would ring the death knell of dollar supremacy. On the other hand, complete U.S. control of oil would preserve the rule of the dollar (not only would oil producers continue to use the dollar for their international trade, but the dollar's international standing would rise) and hurt the credibility of the euro.

In the 1990s the major OPEC countries, after two decades of discouraging or prohibiting foreign investment in oil and gas fields, raced to invite foreign investment again to carry out massive new developments. In the late 1990s Venezuela, Iran, and Iraq struck massive deals with foreign firms for major fields. Even Saudi Arabia invited proposals for development of its untapped natural gas reserves, a move that oil giants responded to with alacrity in the hope the country's mammoth oil fields would also later be opened to foreign investment. However, American firms were shut out of Iran and Iraq by their own government's sanctions; French, Russian, and Chinese firms got the contracts instead. Chavez's increasing assertiveness threatens to shut American firms out of Venezuela as well. The Saudi deal—which the American firms were to lead—stands canceled, apparently because of the Saudi government's fear of public resentment. Thus, if it does not invade the West Asian region, the United States stands to lose dollar hegemony by losing control of the major oil field development projects in the next decade.

3. Oil as a weapon: Direct American control of oil would render potential challengers for world or regional supremacy (Europe's imperialist powers, Japan and China) dependent on the United States. It is clear the United States is following this policy:

- As mentioned above, French, Russian, and Chinese firms will get evicted from Iran and Iraq once the United States troops enter.

- The United States has gone to great lengths to frustrate alternatives to its Baku-Ceyhan pipeline (which is to run from the Caspian region through Turkey to the Mediterranean). With the United States invasion of Afghanistan, the United States has set up a chain of military bases in Central and South Asia—Pakistan, Afghanistan, Kyrgystan, Tajikistan, and Uzbekistan, with military advisers in Georgia as well.

- The United States is about to send two battalions of marines to help suppress the insurgency in Colombia; it is training a new brigade to protect Occidental Petroleum's pipeline in that country. At the same time it is actively organizing the overthrow of the elected Chavez government in Venezuela.

- The Institute for Advanced Strategic and Political Studies, an Israeli lobby group that met President Obasanjo of Nigeria in July 2002, claims the United States is on the verge of a "historic, strategic alignment" with West Africa and that the region is "receptive to American presence." The institute has advocated the setting up of a U.S. Gulf of Guinea military command: the island of Sao Tome, south of Nigeria and a possible site for a naval base, hosted a visit from a U.S. general in the same month. The activity comes while the Nigerian government is considering leaving OPEC and developing its oil trading relationship with the United States instead. The region already provides 15 percent of U.S. oil imports, and these are set to rise to 25 percent by 2015.[51]

- A look at the relative dependence of various imperialist powers on oil imports is revealing. The U.K. is a net oil exporter, thanks to the North Sea. The United States imported, in 2000, 9.8 million barrels a day of its 19.5 million barrel requirement—that is, about half. By contrast, Japan imported 5.5 out of 5.6 million barrels; Germany 2.7 out of 2.8; France 2.0 out of 2.1; Italy 1.8 out of 2.0; and Spain 1.5 out of 1.5.[52] In other words, these countries imported 90 to 100 percent of their oil requirements. *They would therefore be vulnerable to blackmail by a power which is able to dictate the destination of oil.*

  The current U.S. policy is not entirely novel. In the aftermath of World War II, the United States invested large sums in rehabilitating the devastated economies of Europe—what was known as the Marshall Plan. However, it used the plan in order to dictate changes in European economies that made them switch from using their own coal to using oil which American oil majors in West Asia were in the best position to supply.

- *A major consideration in the United States' great oil grab is its desire to check China.* In coming years, China, like the United States, will become a major importer of oil and gas: it is projected to import 10 million barrels a day by 2030—more than 8 percent of world oil demand. (The United States currently imports a little over 10 million barrels of its daily requirement of 20 million barrels.) As China attempts to arrange its future oil supplies, it finds itself checked at each point by the United States:

a.) Since the mid-1990s, China has been pressing for a gas pipeline from the Caspian region to China. With a view to building a security-cum-economic organization for the proposed pipeline, China took the initiative to form a group called the "Shanghai Five" (later six) consisting of China, Russia, and the relevant central Asian states (Kazakhstan, Kyrgyzstan, Tajikistan, and later Uzbekistan). The declared basis for the group was to control fundamentalism and terrorism in the region (stretching to China's westernmost Xinjiang province). However, with the U.S. invasion of Afghanistan, and the installation of its forces in the very countries who were to be in the Shanghai grouping, China's initiative was sabotaged. On a visit to Iran, Chinese president Jiang Zemin declared that "Beijing's policy is against strategies of force and the U.S. military presence in Central Asia and the Middle East region ...." Beijing would work together with developing nations to counter American "hegemonism."[53]

b.) In 2002, Chinese firms bought two Indonesian fields for $585 million and $262 million, respectively. Indonesian president Megawati Sukarnoputri has visited China twice since becoming president in 2001, hoping to bag a $9 billion contract to supply liquid natural gas to power industries in southern China.[54] No surprise that the United States has stepped up its activities in the vicinity of Indonesia—forcing the Philippines to accept its "help" in hunting fundamentalists, patrolling the Malacca Straits in tandem with the Indian navy, and pressing Indonesia to accept U.S. "cooperation" in suppressing Al Qaeda elements in Indonesia itself. A

December 2001 RAND Corporation presentation to a U.S. Congress committee on "threats to the security and stability of Southeast Asia and to U.S. security interests in the region" said that the "primary area of concern is China's emergence as a major regional power.... China's assertiveness will increase as its power grows." It speculated that "conflict could be triggered by energy exploration or exploitation activities," and recommended the creation of a "comprehensive security network in the Asia-Pacific region." Discarding the then U.S. cover that it was hunting for a handful of Abu Sayyaf guerrillas in the Philippines, the RAND Corporation stated: "The United States should provide urgently needed air defense and naval patrol assets to the Philippines to help Manila re-establish deterrence vis-à-vis China and give a further impetus to the revitalization of the United States–Philippines defense relationship.... The United States should expand and diversify its access and support arrangements in Southeast Asia to be able to effectively respond in a timely way to unexpected contingencies. After all, six months ago, who would have thought that U.S. armed forces would be confronted with the need to plan and execute a military campaign in Afghanistan?" The Bali terrorist blast may prove a happy entry point for the United States into Indonesia.

c.) Finally, like the United States, China cannot avoid reliance on West Asian oil. China has struck oil field development deals with the very countries in West Asia hit by U.S. sanctions—Iraq, Iran, Libya,and Sudan. With this entire region now to be targeted in the impending invasion, China's deals are sure to meet the same fate as its central Asian pipeline. Hardly surprising, then, that "Chinese leaders believe that the United States seeks to contain China and [the United States] is therefore a major threat to its [China's] energy security," as the U.S.–China Security Review Commission's report points out.[55]

The thrust is clear: Once it has seized the oil wells of West Asia, the United States will determine not only which firms would bag the deals, not only the currency in which oil trade would be denominated, not only the price of oil on the international market, but even the destination of the oil.

In the Short Term

In the short term, the United States anticipates being in a better position than its rivals to absorb the immediate disruption arising from the war. It seems unlikely that the conventional armed forces of the Iraqi regime— depleted anyway to one-third of their 1990 strength—would pose much of a problem for the United States' initial occupation of Iraq.

While the oil price hike would have an impact on all countries, the United States assesses that it would be in a better position to take the immediate impact of higher oil prices than other countries:

First, it has higher disposable income than the rest of the world, and net energy imports account for just one percent of its GDP. The United States, being a bigger, more powerful economy, can better protect itself from the consequences of the price hike.[56]

Second, compared to other imperialist countries, the United States imports a smaller share of its energy needs. (It also has a strategic petroleum reserve of 580 million barrels—or almost two months' imports.) Moreover, the U.S. economy *depends less on heavy industry* than either the third world or other imperialist countries do, and therefore takes less of a hit when fuel prices rise.

Third, and crucially, at times of international crisis capital docks at safe harbors. The United States anticipates that as it demonstrates its might before the rest of the world, and the world's oil supplies fall into its hands, investors will put their money on the dollar. If the dollar appreciates against other currencies, the United States would feel the impact of the oil price hike less than other countries.[57]

Such a strategy, however, would have a perverse effect even if it succeeds. As the dollar's value rises, American goods would be displaced at home by the then even cheaper imports. U.S. business investment, which has already fallen "virtually to the capital replacement level," would fall even further, shrinking the manufacturing base.[58] The trade deficit—the difference between exports and imports—would widen even further, but the United States would pay for it with inflows of foreign capital seeking security in the powerful dollar. As the values of other currencies fell against the dollar, other economies would be less able to absorb American imports, deepening the manufacturing recession in the United States and the United States trade deficit even further. *The picture is one of consumption without production, dependent on inflows of borrowed foreign capital, which inflows are in turn dependent on American military supremacy.*[59]

Expansion on a Weakening Base

The United States' grand strategy, while portending tremendous upheaval and suffering for the rest of the world, thus has its logic. It is a pattern familiar to students of imperialism: a declining imperialist power relying on military power and possession of colonies to make up for its ebbing economic strength. However, the U.S. military-adventurist course to maintaining its long-term world hegemony is fraught with difficulties that, too, would be familiar to students of imperialism.

There are huge economic costs to a strategy of imperialist expansion on a weakening productive base. Even without a war U.S. military spending swallows 4 percent of the GDP: the U.S. military budget this year is $379 billion, $48 billion over the previous year. By comparison, U.S. military spending during the Cold War (when the United States faced a formidable, nuclear-armed adversary) averaged $347 billion in 2002 dollars.[60]

The cost of an invasion of Iraq is hard to estimate. Estimates put out by the U.S. Congress range from $44 billion to $60 billion. These seem underestimates of even the direct costs. The 1991 assault on Iraq cost $61 billion, of which $48 billion was paid for by U.S. allies. Assuming the impending invasion would cost the same, the bill would come to $80 billion in today's dollars. Moreover, the Congressional Budget Office estimates the costs of military occupation of Iraq at $17 to $45 billion a year, based on the low end of costs of the Kosovo occupation. Further, the United States anticipates invading other states in the region, such as Iran or Saudi Arabia. That would make the war bill an annually recurring feature. Thus direct military spending would rise by around $100 to $200 billion—or another 1 or 2 percent of U.S. GDP.

The required funds would have to be borrowed. This at a time when the U.S. recession is pushing up the U.S. budget deficit. Between spring 2001 and autumn 2002 the annual federal budget deteriorated by $360 billion.

As well-known American economist William D. Nordhaus points out, the broader costs to the United States are much greater: higher oil prices for the period in which supply is disrupted (particularly serious if oil wells are damaged), as well as the psychological effect of uncertainty, which would in turn trigger recession of the order of 2 to 5 percent of GDP. Totaling the direct and indirect costs, Nordhaus arrives at a figure of $120 billion over ten years in a completely favorable case. But he shows that if things go wrong for the United States, the total direct and indirect costs could come to $1.6 trillion over ten years.[61]

Vast Network of Installations

In order to maintain its hegemony over diverse and shifting potential adversaries, the United States is obliged to set up a vast network of military bases. In 1988, the break up of U.S. overseas or foreign bases by region was as follows: 627 in Europe, Canada, and the North Atlantic; 121 in the Pacific and Southeast Asia; 39 in Latin America; 7 in the Middle East and Africa; and zero in South Asia. Of course, there was no question at the time of locating bases in Central Asia which was part of the USSR.[62]

The 1991 assault on Iraq helped bring about the U.S. bases in Saudi Arabia; its intervention in Bosnia, and later its assault on Yugoslavia, brought it bases on the rim of Europe in case Europe should secede from the U.S.-dominated NATO.

Since the invasion of Afghanistan, the picture has changed dramatically. U.S. bases—at first temporary but soon permanent—sprang up in Uzbekistan, Tajikistan, Kyrgyzstan, Afghanistan, and Pakistan, and U.S. military advisers are stationed in Georgia. American naval vessels now regularly visit Indian ports, and a naval base in northern Sri Lanka appears in the offing with the United States intervening in the Tamil national struggle there. "Overall, the American military global presence is more pervasive today than at any point in American history," says John Pike, a military analyst in Washington.[63]

But bases are not enough. The United States needs to suppress the *mass and political forces* that are struggling against it in these diverse regions. To meet this need there is a massive hike in U.S. spending to train foreign militaries—which had already risen steeply during the 1990s (by 1999 U.S. Special Operations Forces were carrying out joint exercises with 152 countries). "It's like the counter-insurgency era all over again," a U.S. congressional aide is quoted as saying, referring to the Vietnam war era. "Only this time we"re going to be fighting 'terrorism' instead of 'communism.'"[64] "On any given day before September 11, according to the Defense Department, more than 60,000 [U.S.] military personnel were conducting temporary operations and exercises in about 100 countries."[65]

The Crucial Roadblock

It is indeed the "counterinsurgency era all over again,"or the *insurgency* era, if we look at it from the point of view of those being attacked by the United States. The growing military assaults by the United States are giving rise to a worldwide protest movement that is in some ways without precedent. It is also giving rise to the anger of greater and greater sections of people. Ironically, the single strong point of the U.S.—its awe-inspiring high-tech military might—has not been able to deliver a thoroughgoing success even in Afghanistan. Rather, its puppet ruler rules just the capital city and that also with the help of foreign troops and U.S. bodyguards, amid growing anti-American sentiment. The anti-U.S. forces are having such obvious success that even *Time* magazine carried a piece titled: "Losing Control? The United States Concedes It Has Lost Momentum in Afghanistan, While Its Enemies Grow Bolder."[66]

In South Korea, where the United States is struggling to retain its bases (that today house 37,000 troops) for targeting China at short notice, an extraordinary mass movement is raging at present calling for U.S. withdrawal from the country. Witness the recent rally of 300,000 in the capital, as well as smaller rallies in other cities.

In the Philippines, the U.S. bases were ousted in the early 1990s through a sustained mass struggle. The fresh efforts to install U.S. forces is already confronting mass protests from a people who were America's first overseas colony.

In Pakistan, the only parliamentary platform campaigning for the removal of American bases made dramatic gains in Musharraf's carefully managed elections. The *New York Times* reports that U.S. plans for a war on Iraq are fueling hatred of the United States in Pakistan. It cites "a recent worldwide opinion poll by the Pew Research Center: 69 percent of Pakistanis held an unfavorable view of the United States and only 10 percent expressed a favorable one. Of the 44 countries surveyed, Pakistan tied with Egypt for the most negative perception of the United States."[67]

Even in Kuwait, as American troops prepare for the invasion of Iraq, they are facing repeated attacks from the population that they supposedly saved in 1991. A Kuwait official is quoted as saying: "The Americans have told us to downplay these incidents for fear of creating the sort of climate in which further attacks can happen."[68]

In Palestine, Israel—the most powerful military power in West Asia—was completely unprepared for the resistance it met in the refugee camp of Jenin. It had to dispatch 10,000 troops and 200 tanks, change commanders five times, and struggle for sixteen days to put down the poorly armed Palestinian defenders. The Palestinians paid homage to their fighters by referring to the town as "Jeningrad"—recalling the heroic battle of Stalingrad that marked the turning point of World War II. Jenin has been turned into rubble, and unknown numbers of Palestinians have been slaughtered; yet there is a seemingly endless stream of Palestinian youth ready to take the place of their dead fellow fighters.

And most striking of all, in Venezuela, it is a month since the pro-U.S. forces have launched their second coup attempt, attempting to prevent the functioning of the oil industry and to paralyze the functioning of the government. They have been answered with a great wave of mass mobilization—completely unreported by the world's giant media corporations—in favor of the Chavez government, indeed in favor of their sovereignty and dignity.

The United States defense secretary has announced that the United States is ready and willing to fight more than one "major theater conflict" *at a time.* As the United States military offensive unfolds in Iraq, in the rest of West Asia, in Colombia, in Venezuela, and in so many other lands, that claim will be put to the test.

The U.S. military juggernaut is still geared to knocking down targets that stand in place, but has a poor record against guerrilla resistance or mass upsurges. As U.S. forces get bogged down in struggles with no clear conclusion or exit, the calculations of the United States' present offensive drive may get unhinged.

For one, the other imperialist powers, now spectators on the sidelines, may take advantage of U.S. difficulties to obtain footholds in the very regions for which the United States is contending. Already the European Union (pressed by France, whose TotalFinaElf is one of the world's five largest oil corporations) has advanced a proposal regarding the Palestinian question that is distinct from the U.S. plan, much to the irritation of the United States. Such intervention may grow as the turmoil intensifies. While these rival powers are out to advance their own imperialist interests, the sharpening of their tussles with the United States will help those facing the immediate brunt of the U.S. attack.

As the U.S. military machine gets tied up in the unending tasks of an occupying power in the third world, the costs—financial and political— will mount. The United States economy, already in recession, may not be in a position to take such weight. U.S. budgetary and trade deficits may veer out of control. Depressed demand conditions in the rest of the world as a result of U.S. policy would boomerang on the United States as it faces less demand for its exports and sharper competition at home for its imports. The U.S. hope that international uncertainty will boost the dollar is only one of two possibilities. It is equally possible that, under the weight of investors" fears that the United States will not be able to service its mounting obligations, a dollar *slide* might take place.

The political costs of a deeper recession are not to be forgotten. Indeed, the entire build up of a vast domestic machinery of repression— under the name of the Office of Homeland Security and the U.S. Patriot

Act—and the whipping up of chauvinism, xenophobia, racism, and fascistic sentiments are in preparation for the possible resistance at home.

A worldwide antiwar movement has already begun. On 28 September 2002 London witnessed its largest rally since the 1930s, encompassing the entire range of society. The attendance of over *four hundred thousand* calling for "Freedom for Palestine" and "Hands off Iraq" constituted a sharp political challenge to the British rulers, junior partners in the U.S. offensive. On the same day, 100,000 rallied in Rome; on the next day, 50,000 in Madrid. The culmination of the protests in Europe, and the largest antiwar rally there, took place on November 8, 2002, in Florence. Many from other parts of Europe joined, as the working people and their unions, political parties, teenagers, students, the elderly, campaigners for the cancellation of third world debt, anti-capitalism activists, artists, intellectuals, and other common people came carrying their banners, placards, and effigies, raising the slogans "No War on Iraq," "No to World War,"and "Bush, Blair and Berlusconi [the Italian prime minister] are murderers."

On October 26, 2002, Washington, San Francisco, and other American cities witnessed the biggest antiwar rallies since the days of the Vietnam War, armed with slogans such as "Dump Bush Not Bombs" and "No Blood for Oil," under the banner "Act Now to Stop War and End Racism (ANSWER)." Apart from the numbers—an estimated 200,000 in Washington alone— three points are worth noting about this protest. First, that it came as part of a whole series of protest actions throughout the country (including a massive April 20 march in Washington in support of the Palestinian people and a very large October 6 antiwar rally in New York City's Central Park). Second, that a large section of the participants were ordinary people who were not part of any organization and may not see themselves as "political." Third, that whereas in the 1960s such large protests were only possible three or four years after the United States sent its troops to Vietnam, they are now being organized *before* the war has started. The antiwar movement is picking up with unanticipated speed.

The exact shape of things to come is hard to predict. Yet it is clear that it is not the sophisticated military technology of the United States, but the response of *people worldwide* that will play the crucial role in determining that shape.

4. REHABILITATING COLONIALISM

A flurry of articles and books has appeared in the United States and U.K. making the case for, or simply announcing, a new type of *colonialism*, or direct rule by an imperial power. The authors, albeit intellectually pedestrian, are important and influential individuals. The sudden emergence of this "new" doctrine is significant: it is part of an explicit attempt to prepare public opinion for mainly U.S. plans in the near future.

The entire history of colonialism, since its emergence five centuries ago, has been marked by points of resistance by the colonized peoples to their subjugation and plunder; but it was the twentieth century that witnessed the great worldwide awakening of the colonial peoples, particularly in the wake of the Russian Revolution of November 1917. The colonial powers responded with exemplary violence, even slaughter. A price in tens of millions of lives all told was paid by the Algerian liberation struggle against French rule, the Indian independence movement, the Chinese people's war against Japanese occupation, the armed struggles of the Indochinese peoples against French rule and the Malay against British rule, the liberation struggles of the peoples of South Africa, Zimbabwe, and Namibia, and many others.

At that terrible price, such struggles shattered the legitimacy of colonialism, and established the right of nations to determine their own future, free from force and imperialist intervention. The struggle took the whole century, with South Africa just in the last decade ending formal white settler rule. Before the Russian Revolution imperialist powers had hardly needed to bother to justify or legitimize colonialism, but after World War I the League of Nations (the predecessor to the United Nations) felt obliged to set up a system of "mandates,"whereby various great powers would "guide" territories that were deemed not yet "ready" for governing themselves. Such disguises for colonialism, too, faced fierce opposition from those who were to be so "guided." Finally, in the second half of the century, imperialism was forced to give up direct rule of the third world.

No doubt the imperialist powers quickly adapted to the new situation by greatly refining and expanding the system of indirect rule, or neo-colonialism, such as they already exercised over some other parts of the world. Indeed, they could in many cases even intensify exploitation under such arrangements. But they were never reconciled to giving up the *option* of direct rule. Even when, as in Vietnam, the United States sent in troops and effectively occupied the country, it felt compelled to set up a puppet regime in whose defense it claimed to be fighting.

Today, basking in the warm glow of its unchallenged global supremacy, the United States has felt confident to set up *near-colonial* arrangements in certain countries. What else could one call the outcome of the conflicts in former Yugoslavia, where the administration of Bosnia is run by an appointed High Representative, not a Bosnian; the soldiers who guard the region are foreigners (Europeans and Americans); and police, judges, prison officers, even central bankers—are foreigners? The territory's local police are financed and trained by the UN. Elections are organized and monitored by the Organization for Security and Cooperation in Europe (OSCE).

After the NATO assault on Yugoslavia in 1999, the Bosnian set up was replicated for Kosovo. In the wake of its invasion of Afghanistan, the United States has installed a near-colonial arrangement in that country, too. And now, as we shall see below, it appears that the United States has plans for going even further in parts of West Asia, beginning with Iraq.

Justifying the New Colonizing Mission

Hardly coincidental, then, that a group of influential apologists and "theoreticians" for a new bout of colonialism has suddenly emerged. In the American media, they include *Wall Street Journal* editorial features editor Max Boot, *Washington Post* columnist Sebastian Mallaby, *Newsweek* columnist Charles Krauthammer, and *Atlantic Monthly* essayist Robert Kaplan; in American academia, Johns Hopkins University foreign policy expert Charles Fairbanks, Harvard professor of human rights policy Michael Ignatieff, the head of the Olin Institute for Strategic Studies at Harvard University, Stephen Peter Rosen, and Georgetown University Professor of Geopolitics and Global Justice G. John Ikenberry. In Britain they include prime minister Tony Blair's foreign affairs adviser Robert Cooper, chief economic commentator of the *Financial Times* (London) Martin Wolf, and historian Paul Johnson.[1]

The theoretical justification, such as it is, provided by Cooper (and parroted by Wolf) is that advanced states face a threat from "premodern states" such as Afghanistan. The former can disregard the national sovereignty of the latter, since "the premodern world is a world of failed states. Here the state no longer fulfills Weber's criterion of having the monopoly on the legitimate use of force." Cooper includes vast vague swathes of the world in this category: "Some areas of the former Soviet Union... including Chechnya. All of the world's major drug-producing areas.... Until recently there was no real sovereign authority in Afghanistan; nor is there in up-country Burma or in some parts of South America.... All over Africa countries are at risk. No area of the world is without its dangerous cases."

How can such feeble regimes pose a threat to the world's most powerful countries? Cooper surmounts this awkward hurdle by arguing that such regimes "can provide a base for non-state actors who may represent a danger to the postmodern [advanced] world.... If they become too dangerous for established states to tolerate, it is possible to imagine a defensive imperialism."

Interestingly, not only security conditions in the failed states but even the failure of such states to follow *economic* policies promoted by the advanced countries appears to justify colonization. Cooper frets that "the need for colonization is as great as it ever was in the nineteenth century. Those left out of the global economy risk falling into a vicious circle. Weak government means disorder and that means falling investment" and thereby, presumably, chaos. Cooper calls for "a world in which the efficient and well-governed export stability and liberty, and which [world] is open for investment and growth." Martin Wolf describes a "failed state" as afflicted with, among other things, "inefficient economic policies aimed at favoring particular groups. High fiscal deficits, inflation, costly protection against imports and repression of the financial system...."

According to Wolf, "If a failed state is to be rescued, the essential parts of honest government—above all *the coercive apparatus*—must be provided from outside" (emphasis added). Cooper says, "*The most logical way to deal with chaos, and the one most employed in the past is colonization.* But today, he acknowledges, it would require better packaging: "What is needed then is a new kind of imperialism, one acceptable to a world of human rights and cosmopolitan values."[2]

The hub of the current colonial apologetics is in the United States. Here there is not talk of a "defensive imperialism." Rather, empire is a *positive mission.* Charles Krauthammer bluntly calls for a "new imperium." Kaplan's book *Warrior Politics* argues for a crusade "to bring prosperity to distant parts of the world under America's soft imperial influence." According to Kaplan, "There's a positive side to empire. It's in some ways the most benign form of order." Ikenberry as well sees America's "imperial goals and modus operandi" as "benign." Far blunter is former national security adviser Zbigniew Brzezinski, who describes the main task of the United States in the preservation of its empire as being "*to prevent collusion and maintain dependence among the vassals, to keep tributaries pliant and protected, and to keep the barbarians from coming together*" (emphasis added).

Necessary to having an empire is the ability to declare that it is yours, so quite naturally the Americans are fed up with lingering inhibitions in this regard. "People are now coming out of the closet on the word 'empire,'" says Krauthammer. "The fact is no country has been as dominant culturally, economically, technologically, and militarily in the history of the world since the Roman Empire." As John Bellamy Foster points out, in stark contrast to the past, when using the word *imperialist* would mark one as a leftist, now "U.S. intellectuals and the political elite are warmly embracing an openly 'imperialist' or 'neoimperialist' mission for the United States, repeatedly enunciated in such prestigious print media as the *New York Times* and *Foreign Affairs*." The words *empire* and *imperialism* have regained academic respectability: Johns Hopkins University foreign policy expert Charles Fairbanks calls the United States "an empire in formation"; Stephen Peter Rosen, head of the Olin Institute for Strategic Studies at Harvard University, writes, "Our goal [that of the American military] is not combating a rival, but maintaining our imperial position, and maintaining imperial order."

The brazenness is startling. In his article "The Case for American Empire," where he calls for the military occupation of Afghanistan and Iraq, Max Boot of the *Wall Street Journal* invokes the legacy of the British imperial past: "Afghanistan and other troubled lands today cry out for the sort of enlightened foreign administration once provided by self-confident Englishmen in jodhpurs and pith helmets." The historian Paul Johnson, writing in the *Wall Street Journal*, envisages a sprawling direct empire:

America and her allies may find themselves, temporarily at least, not just occupying with troops but administering obdurate terrorist states. These may eventually include not only Afghanistan but Iraq, Sudan, Libya, Iran, and Syria. Democratic regimes willing to abide by international law [read: the will of the United States] will be implanted where possible, but a Western political presence seems unavoidable in some cases.

According to the apologists of U.S. superpower politics, once American troops occupied a country, the earlier "terrorist state" presumably would no longer exist; so whence the continuing "obduracy" in those states? What is left unstated is that the *people* of the country might continue to resist, making American military rule "unavoidable."

The United States is evidently contemplating devising international legal instruments for legitimizing such arrangements. Well-known establishment intellectuals of the breed cited above do not merely in some general way reflect the mood of the times or ruling class interests: they also reflect specific discussions with senior officials and politicians. Perhaps this explains the uncanny coincidence of their views. Wolf considers that "some form of United Nations temporary protectorate can surely be created"; Boot wants to revive the League of Nations "mandate" system; and Johnson chimes in:

> I suspect the best medium-term solution will be to revive the old League of Nations mandate system, which served well as a "respectable" form of colonialism between the wars. Syria and Iraq were once highly successful mandates. Sudan, Libya, and Iran have likewise been placed under special regimes by international treaty. Countries that cannot live at peace with their neighbors and wage covert war against the international community cannot expect total independence. With all the permanent members of the Security Council now backing, in varying degrees, the American-led initiative, it should not be difficult to devise a new form of United Nations mandate that places terrorist states under responsible supervision.

A glance at the behavior of the United States during the last year confirms that Wolf, Boot, Johnson, and their ilk reflect current official thinking.

Afghanistan

Here the present regime was installed after a U.S.-led invasion. The interim head of state was hand-picked by the United States (having proved his credentials earlier as an employee of an American multinational and later as an asset of the Central Intelligence Agency). The budget of the government consists of foreign aid. On January 29, the IMF's assistant director for monetary and exchange affairs suggested that the country should abandon its currency and adopt the dollar instead as a "temporary" measure. The country's central bank is run by the IMF and World Bank. Textbooks for Afghanistan's schools are being prepared in an American university. The BBC is helping to set up media operations in the country.

An international force under American direction polices the capital. The *Times of India* reported that the United States and its tail the U.K. demanded that the force have an open-ended mandate under Chapter VII of the UN Charter, allowing them to undertake coercive operations, make arrests and use force in situations other than just self-defense. Washington also wants the UN-mandated force to function under the overall control of the U.S. army's Central Command (Centcom). This would allow the force to dovetail its activities to the wider U.S. military campaign in Afghanistan, which Washington says will continue even though Al Qaeda and the Taliban no longer control territory. As for duration, the United States and Britain want an open-ended tenure rather than the early sunset clause favored by Russia and France.... Mr. Abdullah [foreign minister-designate], in fact, had told the UN Security Council the international force should have a Chapter VI mandate allowing it to use force only in self-defense. Under U.S. pressure, however, Mr. Karzai overruled Mr. Abdullah and assented to the tougher Chapter VI mandate giving the force—which Britain declared unilaterally that it would lead—a freer hand.[3]

In March 2002 it was announced that the United States was to help fund and train the new Afghan army. The assessment of the requirements of this force was carried out by the chief of staff of the U.S. Central Command.

Meanwhile the United States continues war operations in various parts of the country without reference to the supposed government of the country. On December 4, 2001, Richard Haass, the director of the U.S. State Department's policy planning staff, said he saw "no problem in us continuing the war even as the new interim authority goes about its business."

On December 20, acting on information from a warlord, Washington bombed a convoy of pro-Karzai village elders traveling to Kabul to attend Karzai's inauguration. As the survivors scrambled up a hill toward two villages, the planes circled back and bombed the two villages, killing 42.

On December 29, U.S. planes bombed Qala Niazi village, slaughtering, according to a UN spokeswoman, 52 villagers. At this point defense minister Mohammed Fahim called for a halt to the U.S. bombing. Village elders in eastern Afghanistan complained that hundreds of villagers were being killed. However, the following day the chairman of the interim government, Hamid Karzai, voiced his support for the bombing campaign.

The U.S. special envoy to Afghanistan said that while he regretted the civilian casualties ("war is a very imperfect business"), bombing would go on until the goals were met.

On January 30, U.S. Special Forces killed 16 officials of the regime in a district and took 27 prisoner. The Afghan "government," such as it is, protested that the victims were their own officials, including the district police chief, but the Pentagon merely reasserted that they were a legitimate target.

On July 1, 2002, on the suspicion that Taliban leaders were attending a wedding in Kakarak in Uruzgan province, U.S. planes bombed four villages, slaughtering over 60 innocent villagers, wiping out whole families in a night. In the morning, U.S. forces entered the village, stormed houses, tied the hands of men and women, and did not allow people to help the victims, take them for treatment or even cover the dead bodies, from which the clothes had been burned. Apparently for U.S. military records, the soldiers filmed and photographed the dead bodies, including those of the women.[4]

The Kakarak episode put the Karzai regime under pressure. Hundreds of Afghans (half of them women) marched in Kabul to protest the killings—an unprecedented development. Karzai huddled with the commander of the allied forces in Afghanistan, Lt. Gen. Dan K. McNeill. The Afghan foreign minister called for a role for the Afghan "government" in deciding about the air strikes.

These pleas were ignored, the Pentagon defended its action, and the United States continued its strikes. As one of the Kakarak survivors said to a correspondent, "Karzai is just a traffic cop working for the Americans."

There could hardly be a more striking expression of the isolation and dependence of the present regime than "President" Karzai's decision in July to remove his earlier bodyguards and replace them with American troops. "We know there could be a great political cost from doing this," said a Western diplomat, "but that price, no matter how much, will be less than losing the president" (not attempting to hide that Karzai was his country's property to "lose"). Karzai is not alone: a core of senior ministers has also adopted U.S. bodyguards. In August the United States announced that responsibility for Karzai's security would now be taken over by the U.S. State Department diplomatic security service for at least a year.

An attempt was made to confer some sort of legitimacy on Karzai by arranging a *loya jirga*, a traditional assembly or parliament of delegates of the various tribes and communities in Afghanistan, to pick a new government. The delegates were carefully screened to exclude all troublesome elements. Nevertheless, at the affair itself, some 60-70 delegates walked out in protest at the proceedings. Some delegates pointed out that the number of participants was 1,700, instead of 1,500 "elected" delegates as announced, and among the extra, unelected participants were many warlords and their henchmen. "Many tribal delegates ... expressed concern at 'outside influence' overshadowing the event. All were aware *the American envoy Zalmay Khalilzad, had been the first to announce* the former king would stay out of government, after intense backroom politicking delayed the assembly opening by some twenty-four hours. The king's decision means Mr. Karzai has no serious challenger as president. 'This is not a democracy,' Sima Samar, the women's affairs minister, said yesterday. 'This is a rubber stamp. Everything has already been decided by the powerful ones.'"[5]

Pakistan

In Afghanistan the U.S. was fortunate to find a country in the sort of "chaos" that, according to Cooper, justifies colonial takeover. The situation in Pakistan is very different, yet there too U.S. behavior smacks of the imperial ruler dealing with what Brzezinski terms "vassals." This is not a new development, but since September 11 the situation has worsened dramatically:

> In the immediate aftermath of 9/11, Mr. Powell decided that Pakistan was bound to be the linchpin if the United States was to take on the Al Qaeda on its turf. He and Mr. Armitage drew up a list of seven demands for Pakistan: stop Al Qaeda operatives at the border, intercept arms shipments and end all logistical support for Bin Laden; provide blanket overflight and landing rights; access to Pakistan naval bases, air bases and borders; immediate intelligence and immigration information; condemn the September 11 attacks and *curb all domestic expression of support for terrorism against the United States*, its friends and allies; *cut off all shipments of fuel to the Taliban* [making it

impossible to get food supplies to about seven million without food] and stop Pakistani volunteers from going into Afghanistan to join the Taliban; break diplomatic relations with the Taliban and assist the United States to destroy Bin Laden and his Al Qaeda network.[6]

Quite apart from the surrender of sovereignty in other respects, the directive to curb all domestic expression of support for "terrorism" against the United States constituted a takeover of Pakistani political life. As American air strikes began on October 7, Pakistan was rocked by repeated protests against the assault on Afghanistan. The Pakistani government responded with vigorous repression. On October 9 police fired killing three protesters in Kuchlak town; on October 12 tear gas was fired at protesters in Karachi; on October 14 three persons were killed in firing on thousands of protesters at Jacobabad, where U.S. forces were stationed (even as the Pakistani government denied their presence); October 15 witnessed a general strike in Pakistan against Powell's visit; on October 23 the government was forced to seal off Jacobabad town to prevent an attempt by people to surround the base; on October 24 Karachi witnessed a stormy funeral gathering for 35 Harkat militants killed by a U.S. bomb in Kabul; and Agence France Presse reported that an October 26 rally in the same city mobilized 50,000. By this point Musharraf, obediently implementing the American directive to "curb all domestic expressions of support" to the Taliban, had detained thousands nationwide, including most of the prominent political leaders opposing the United States invasion of Afghanistan.

According to a survey taken in October 2001 by the American polling organization Gallup, 83 percent of Pakistanis said they supported the Taliban; 82 percent termed Osama bin Laden a *mujahid* (a just warrior) and not a terrorist; and 75 percent opposed Musharraf's decision to allow the United States to use Pakistani bases.[7] In other words, Musharraf had to curb (in fact, suppress) the expression of opinions held by the overwhelming majority of his citizens.

To help the United States prosecute its so-called war against terror, Pakistan has signed a "defense" pact which allowed U.S. forces to replenish their supplies via its territory and to use its facilities for training, joint military exercises, and other operations. Thanks to the invasion of Afghanistan, the United States now has acquired four bases in the Pakistan—Jacobabad, Shamsi, Dalbandin, and Pasni (on the coast)—without any formal invasion of Pakistan.

The entire police, security, and intelligence apparatus of Pakistan is being openly subordinated to the United States, and the loyalty of its personnel to the new masters is being checked. On December 3, immediately following the visit of George Tenet, the director of the U.S. Central Intelligence Agency (CIA), Pakistan's law minister Shahida Jamil said that the United States, the EU, and Japan were providing "professional training" to Pakistani security forces and will provide modern investigation facilities. The Asian Development Bank had promised a *$350 million* three-year concessional loan for "police and judicial reforms." The *Times of India* reported that "Mr. Tenet's visit will result in greater U.S. intelligence and law enforcement presence in Pakistan to keep track of *jehadi* elements and organizations. Already, the FBI has been deployed at major Pakistani airports to monitor the movement of *jehadis* and terrorists."[8]

According to an American news channel, Pakistan has signed a secret agreement with the United States to allow hot pursuit of Al Qaeda fighters over the border with Afghanistan. The secret deal will allow U.S. troops to hunt the fighters on the ground and fire on them from the air within Pakistan's borders.[9] In April the Pakistani press reported that U.S. troops were operating in the country. This was denied by Pakistani officials. A foreign ministry spokesman said that when President Musharraf said there were "some (U.S.) officials inside Pakistan for communicating purposes," he was referring to "a few members" of the FBI. Meanwhile, in the United States, officials acknowledged that U.S. Special Forces were chasing Al Qaeda or Taliban in Pakistan.

In the past, even the Pakistani army had never policed the fiercely independent tribal areas of the northwest frontier, but had left it to the tribes themselves. However, the United States now dictated otherwise. In May, the Pakistani paper *The News* reported Pakistani officials' pleas to

U.S. assistant secretary of state Christina Rocca that the United States stop carrying out direct raids in tribal areas. They asked that Pakistani troops be used instead. It appears, from a report of September 2002, that the Pakistani army is now carrying out operations in these regions "with the support of U.S. agencies,"hunting for Al Qaeda/Taliban.

As the U.S. presence grows in the region, Islamic militants have stepped up their attacks on foreigners in Pakistan. This in turn has provided an excuse for U.S. agencies to expand their presence further. Whether after the March 19 bombing of an Islamabad church in which two members of American diplomats' families were among those killed, the May 9 Karachi bombing in which French submarine engineers (but no Americans) were killed, or the car bombing outside the U.S. consulate in Karachi, in the investigations into all of these incidents the FBI was directly involved, inspecting the site and questioning suspects along with the Pakistani police.

Indeed the FBI is now involved not only in "investigation" but *even in hunting down suspects and making arrests within Pakistan.* On September 14, 2002, Ramzi bin al-Shibh, claimed to be an important Al Qaeda leader, was arrested in Karachi in a joint FBI-CIA-Pakistani operation. "The FBI and Pakistani intelligence agencies are investigating them," said senior police officer. "*The FBI and Pakistan ISI had initially raided the place* and arrested two suspects, but later the police were called out to help in the operation when other suspects present in the building retaliated."[10] Ramzi bin al-Shibh was then handed over to the United States to be transported to their concentration camp in Guantanamo, Cuba. The same fate had some months earlier befallen another Al Qaeda operative, Abu Zubaydah.

In the past, Pakistan had handed over Ramzi Yousef (suspect in the 1993 bombing of the World Trade Center) and Aimal Kasi (who shot two CIA employees in the United States in 1993) *without any formal extradition,* which would require a legal process within Pakistan. However, the present traffic is on a much larger scale. On June 19, Amnesty International pointed out that Pakistan was "flouting its own laws and violating human rights by arresting and deporting hundreds of people from Pakistan in pursuit of the U.S.-led "war on terrorism." "Pakistan," said Amnesty, "is making arbitrary arrests and sending suspects back to their home countries to face possible torture and execution. The rule of law has been swept aside. Detainees are not treated in accordance with either Pakistani or international law. Human rights protection has been thrown out the window. Who is being held where is unknown. Detainees are cut off from family and lawyers and there are no official notices."

Clearly, Pakistan is not preparing the lists of persons to deport. All this is being done under the direction of, indeed in the physical presence of, American agencies. The United States, having kidnapped such persons from Pakistan with the help of the Pakistani state, thereafter keeps them in legal limbo and in appalling conditions in a Guantanamo concentration camp, perhaps even torturing them with sophisticated means. When the United States finds that it no longer has any use for some of them, it returns them like so much waste paper to Pakistan, with the comment that they could not be connected to terrorism. The United States has similarly deported some of the Pakistani citizens whom it has detained within the United States as part of its nationwide arbitrary roundup of Muslims. *Pakistan accepts them all back without a murmur* ; not even the pretense of sovereignty or representation of its citizens is permitted.

The United States is showing impatience with the Pakistani legal system, including the judiciary. The release of a Lashkar-e-Toiba leader by a Pakistan court on November 20, 2002, because he had been unlawfully detained, drew the warning from U.S. State Department deputy spokesman Philip Reeker that "Pakistani law enforcement agencies, just like law enforcement agencies around the world, must ensure that those responsible for terrorist crimes are brought to justice." Presumably the necessary changes will be covered in the $350 million package for police and judicial reform.

The United States plans to reshape not only the administration of Pakistan but Pakistani society itself. It has demanded changes in, or the closing down, of the *madrassas*, the traditional Islamic schools that it now considers training grounds for anti-American militancy. It was not an American aid agency but the United States national security adviser,

Condoleezza Rice, who announced on February 1: "We are moving quickly with places like Pakistan, to help them improve their educational system."

"Reform" extends to the political system as well. Musharraf's farcical, rigged election—for a parliament he has the right to dismiss at whim—turned up an unexpected result. The pro-Musharraf Pakistan Muslim League (Qaid-e-Azam) did not win a majority, but the Muttahida Majlis-e-Amal (MMA), a conglomeration of Islamic parties (headed by the same persons who had been detained during the invasion of Afghanistan), campaigning on an anti-U.S. platform, won a large number of seats. Since no party won a majority, the MMA had to be considered as a partner in forming a government, but U.S. intervention prevented it from assuming that role:

> Three weeks of heavy bargaining and behind-the-scenes activity have enabled President General Pervez Musharraf to split the Pakistan People's Party and secure support for the PML (Q)-led government.... General Musharraf, according to Pakistan newspaper reports, along with the rest of the establishment had underestimated the influence of the MMA, assuring the Americans at one stage that it would not secure more than 6 percent of the vote. The unprecedented results were a surprise to MMA leaders with the group emerging as a major factor in government formation. An initial move by General Musharraf to accommodate the MMA in a coalition government was reportedly scuttled by the United States with anti-American statements from its leaders being received with great consternation in Washington. In the three weeks of fast-moving developments, the PPP also worked out an initial understanding with the MMA. Reports available here suggest that Ms. Bhutto was invited for discussions with U.S. interlocutors and after the meetings did not pursue this alliance.[11]

Palestine

The new brazen colonial attitude is equally on display in recent statements regarding Palestine. On June 25 the American president baldly called for the Palestinians to throw out the president of the Palestinian Authority, Yasser Arafat, pending which they could not hope for a state of their own: "Peace requires a new and different Palestinian leadership, so that a Palestinian state can be born. I call on the Palestinian people to elect new leaders not compromised by terror.... When the Palestinian people have new leaders, new institutions and new security arrangements with their neighbors, the United States of America will support the creation of a new Palestinian state." Two days later, Bush warned that financial aid too was contingent on sacking Arafat: "I've got confidence in the Palestinians, when they understand fully what we're saying, that they'll make the right decisions.... I can assure you, we won't be putting money into a society which is not transparent and [is] corrupt, and I suspect other countries won't either."

The U.S. secretary of state Colin Powell confirmed this was the official U.S. stand: progress toward a settlement "must begin with reform within the Palestinian leadership. To move forward it is absolutely clear that the first step on the road map has to be reformed Palestinian leadership that can then bring the terror under control." National security adviser Condoleezza Rice grimly warned Palestinians that they must be aware of the consequences of their choice: "The United States respects the democratic processes, but if a leadership emerges that does not deal with terrorism, the United States cannot deal with that.... Until there is that change [along the lines desired by the United States], a change that we are prepared to help actively bring about through international assistance, we are not going to be able to make progress on peace."

Magnanimously, Powell said he would be "more than willing to consider" retaining Arafat as a figurehead above a prime minister with real power. Nor was this a casual remark: Saeb Erekat, the chief Palestinian negotiator, later revealed that in a Washington meeting Powell and Rice proposed that the Palestinian parliament implement such a formula. "We were shocked during the discussions," said Erekat, "that the American side is speaking about changing the law of elections." The United States, he said, was trying to delay the balloting in order to give time for this.

All this despite Arafat's years of prostration before the United States and meekness before Israeli terrorism. Indeed, in response Arafat desperately denied that Bush's remarks referred to him, and wrote Powell a long letter describing the 100-day "democratic reform program" he had introduced—even as the latter simply refused to meet him at all. The "reform" program appears to have been drawn up in June by the chief of the CIA during a visit to the region on a "mission to reshape Palestinian security services into a body that can restore some order."[12]

As a first step, Arafat made changes in his cabinet, but these were contemptuously dismissed by the United States. "You can say we are underwhelmed. This does not complete the process of what needs to be done," said a State Department Official.[13] Washington was particularly annoyed that one of its favorites, interior minister Abdel-Razzak al-Yahya, was dropped.

Broader Designs

Palestinians are facing today what much of West Asia will face tomorrow. American plans for the region are sweeping. According to a report in the *Washington Post*, the Bush administration plans to launch a project for "promoting economic, education, and political reforms in West Asia." It would include funds for training political activists and journalists. The *Post* said that the September 11 attacks gave voice to advocates within the administration who favored "democracy-building" programs in West Asia. "It's this whole change in the parameters of how we look at West Asia, that it's no longer off limits," said a senior State Department official. "The state of affairs in these countries has to be a matter of interest to us."[14]

As we have discussed elsewhere in this issue, the dominant section of the Bush administration, led by Vice President Cheney, has plans to reshape the entire region:

> As the Bush administration debates going to war against Iraq, its most hawkish members are pushing a sweeping vision for the Middle East that sees the overthrow of President Saddam Hussein of Iraq as merely a first step in the region's transformation.

Cheney revealed some of the thinking in a speech in August when he made the administration's case for a regime change. He argued Hussein's overthrow would "bring about a number of benefits to the region" and enhance U.S. ability to advance the Israeli-Palestinian peace process. "When the gravest of threats are eliminated, the freedom-loving peoples of the region will have a chance to promote the values that can bring lasting peace," he told the national convention of the Veterans of Foreign Wars.[15]

Among the proposals being discussed (and reported in the American press) are *the invasion of Iran and Syria* (two regimes that have not yet buckled to the United States), the takeover of Saudi Arabia, an American ally with a U.S. military base, and *Egypt*, whose leaders are the United States' most faithful servants in the region. Meanwhile, *Israel has serious plans to drive the Palestinian population of the occupied territories into neighboring Jordan*, ruled by an American client Hashemite monarchy. Jordan might also be one of the routes through which the United States would launch the assault on Iraq. As a bribe, Jordan might be given some figurehead status in Iraq (a member of the Hashemite family ruled over Iraq till he was overthrown in 1958).

We have discussed these proposals elsewhere in this text. These remain proposals, not final decisions. Here we mention them to indicate the *massive expansion of direct imperialist occupation* being contemplated.

No doubt this is occasionally clothed as spreading "democracy" in the region. While Bush has stated quite bluntly, and ad nauseam, "It is the stated policy of this government to have a regime change in Iraq," Condoleezza Rice says the United States will then be "completely devoted" to the reconstruction of Iraq as a "unified, democratic state."

By "democracy" she means American military dictatorship, as revealed by a remarkable article in the *New York Times*, which is worth quoting at length. All pretenses are dropped:

The White House is developing a detailed plan, modeled on the postwar occupation of Japan, to install an American-led military government in Iraq if the United States topples Saddam Hussein, senior administration officials said today. The plan also calls for war crime trials of Iraqi leaders and a transition to an elected civilian government that could take months or years.

In the initial phase, *Iraq would be governed by an American military commander*, perhaps Gen. Tommy R. Franks, commander of United States forces in the Persian Gulf, or one of his subordinates....

In contemplating an occupation, the administration is scaling back the initial role for Iraqi opposition forces in a post-Hussein government. Until now it had been assumed that Iraqi dissidents both inside and outside the country would form a government, but it was never clear when they would take full control. Today marked the first time the administration has discussed what could be a lengthy occupation by coalition forces, led by the United States.

Officials say they want to avoid the chaos and in fighting that have plagued Afghanistan since the defeat of the Taliban. Mr. Bush's aides say they also want full control over Iraq while American-led forces carry out their principal mission: finding and destroying weapons of mass destruction.

Asked what would happen if American pressure prompted a coup against Mr. Hussein, a senior official said, "That would be nice." But the official suggested that the *American military might enter and secure the country anyway*, not only to eliminate weapons of mass destruction but also to ensure against anarchy....

For as long as the coalition partners administered Iraq, they would essentially control the second largest proven reserves of oil in the world, nearly 11 percent of the total.

Administration officials said they were moving away from the model used in Afghanistan: establishing a provisional government right away that would be run by Iraqis. Some top Pentagon officials support this approach, but the State Department, the Central Intelligence Agency, and, ultimately, the White House, were cool to it. "We're just not sure what influence groups on the outside would have on the inside," an administration official said. "There would also be differences among Iraqis, and we don't want chaos and anarchy in the early process...."

In a speech on Saturday, Zalmay Khalilzad, the special assistant to the president for Near East, Southwest Asian, and North African affairs, said, "The coalition will assume... responsibility for the territorial defense and security of Iraq after liberation. Our intent is not conquest and occupation of Iraq. But we do what needs to be done to achieve the disarmament mission and to get Iraq ready for a democratic transition *and then through democracy over time.*"

Iraqis, perhaps through a consultative council, would assist an American-led military and, later, a civilian administration, a senior official said today. Only after this transition would the American-led government hand power to Iraqis. He said that the Iraqi armed forces would be "downsized," and that senior Ba'ath Party officials who control government ministries would be removed. "Much of the bureaucracy would carry on under new management," he added.[16]

The course of this new colonizing mission, however, is unlikely to run smooth, for three reasons.

First, as in earlier colonialism, the present mission is aimed not only at intensifying the plunder of third world countries but at denying other imperialist countries space at the feeding trough (as discussed elsewhere).

Secondly, as James K. Galbraith writes, "There is a reason for the vulnerability of empires. To maintain one against opposition requires war—steady, unrelenting, unending war." Galbraith points out that the current prosperity of the United States "does not mean that we have the financial or material capacity to wage continuing war around the world. Even without war, Bush is already pushing the military budget up toward $400 billion per year. That's a bit more than 4 percent of the current gross domestic product. A little combat—on, say, the Iraqi scale—could raise this figure by another $100 billion to $200 billion. A large-scale war such as might break out in a general uprising through the Middle East or South Asia, with the control of nuclear arsenals at stake, would cost much more and could continue for a long time."[17] In the middle of a grave recession with no end in sight, such a development could have a profound effect on the American economy.

Thirdly, as the American empire spreads, and its physical presence sprawls across the globe, it finds it increasingly difficult to focus on and crush the multiplying points of resistance. An alert piece in the *Christian Science Monitor* picks up the trend:

As the United States gears up to expand Washington's "war on terror" to Iraq, a series of fresh attacks against U.S. forces ... underscores the risk to growing U.S. military deployments.

From Kuwait and Afghanistan to South Korea and the Philippines, U.S. forces have been recently targeted in ways that seem to bear out, even if partially, fresh promises by Al Qaeda and its supporters to continue their war against America.

Even before an Iraq strike, U.S. forces seem to be coming under increasing fire even in nations that are strong allies. In Afghanistan, U.S. forces continuing their operations in the east of the country, especially around the former Taliban and Al Qaeda stronghold of Khost, have been hit by frequent gun, rocket, and mortar fire.

U.S. soldiers conducting pursuit operations across the border in Pakistan—a key U.S. ally throughout the Afghan campaign—are also reported to have come under rocket fire in recent months.

U.S. troops deployed in the Philippines last spring to help the Manila government overcome Abu Sayyaf guerrillas.... Last week, a bombing conducted by a man on a motorcycle killed one American soldier and wounded 23 people outside an open-air restaurant and karaoke bar near a military camp occupied by U.S. and Philippine troops in the city of Zamboanga, some 500 miles south of Manila.

In Korea, where 37,000 U.S. troops are deployed, an angry mob last month briefly abducted an American soldier and forced him to make apologies in a university stadium over an incident last June in which two Korean girls were accidentally run over by a U.S. armored vehicle.

Such incidents are growing as U.S. forces expand operations to include deployments in the former Soviet republics of Georgia, Uzbekistan, and Kyrgyzstan, and even to Djibouti and Yemen.[18]

History does not, cannot, repeat itself; for all the actors and the political context have changed in the course of historical developments. The enduring legacy of the great anti-colonial struggles is the anti-imperialist consciousness of the people of the world, who refuse—whatever the weaknesses of their organization—to submit to subjugation.

NOTES

2. WESTERN IMPERIALISM AND IRAQ

1. A "concession" is a piece of territory that the host country has allowed a company to occupy or use in a particular way, usually for a sum of money. Historically, concessions typically have been granted for railways, mines, and ports.
2. Edward Greer, "The Hidden History of the Iraq War," *Monthly Review*, May 1991.
3. The United States did not then require Iraqi oil for its own consumption: large finds on its mainland by the 1930s created a glut of capacity. American oil companies needed an overseas presence in order to *restrict* global supply and thus maintain prices that would be profitable to them. And the United States, as the new leader of the capitalist world, wanted to ensure that the world's strategic resources came under its control. Later, after World War II, the United States would use its control of West Asian oil as one of its instruments for dominating Europe.
4. Joe Stork, *Middle East Oil and the Energy Crisis* (New York: Monthly Review Press, 1975), p. 14.
5. The interchangeability of Big Oil and government personnel is a tradition of U.S. political life, with predictable effects; in the current administration, President Bush, Vice President Cheney, and National Security Adviser Condoleezza Rice are all former oil company executives.
6. Michael Tanzer, *The Energy Crisis, World Struggle for Power and Wealth* (New York: Monthly Review Press, 1974), p. 59.
7. Stork, *Middle East Oil and the Energy Crisis*, p. 119.
8. The French and the Dutch continued to be part owners, but remained in the background; France in particular was seen by Iraq as sympathetic to Iraqi concerns.
9. The Organization of Petroleum Exporting Countries (OPEC) was founded in Baghdad in September 1960 to unify and coordinate member states' petroleum policies. The original members included Iraq, Iran, Kuwait, Saudi Arabia, and Venezuela.
10. Tanzer, *The Energy Crisis*, p.52.
11. Stork, *Middle East Oil and the Energy Crisis*, p. 194; passim, for much of the above.
12. The fact that the United States considered Iraq's secularism a buffer against Khomeini's "Islamic revolution" makes a hash of the occasional U.S. attempts today to paint Saddam as an ally of a global Islamic fundamentalist conspiracy.
13. *New York Times*, 18 August 2002.

14. That is, slipped from U.S. control.

15. *Times of India*, 2 October 2002.

16. Alan Simpson, MP, and Dr. Glen Rangwala, "The Dishonest Case for War on Iraq," *Labour Against the War Counter-Dossier*, 17 September 2002.

17. Kuwait, with the consent of its ruler, became part of Basra province under the Ottoman Empire in 1871. However, it was made a separate protectorate by the British when they occupied Iraq after World War I. When the British gave Iraq "independence" in 1932 they did not include Kuwait in its territory. It was only in 1961 that they withdrew from the oil-rich and strategically located pocket of Kuwait. Hemmed in on one side by Iran and on the other by Kuwait, Iraq's access to the sea is tiny and vulnerable.

18. *New York Times International*, 23 September 1990; all emphasis added.

19. Ibid.; emphasis added

20. The United States used falsified satellite photographs to convince the Saudis that Iraqi troops were massed at the Saudi border and about to attack their country; this helped overcome Saudi worries about the stationing of non-Muslim troops in the lands of Mecca and Medina.

21. The United States secured passage of Resolution 678 via an exceptionally ruthless campaign of bribery and threats. Every impoverished country on the Security Council, including Zaire, Ethiopia, and Colombia, was offered low-cost oil and the resumption of military aid suspended as a result of human rights violations. After Yemen cast one of two votes in opposition to the Resolution (Cuba was the other), an open microphone captured the United States ambassador telling the Yemeni representative: "That was the most expensive vote you ever cast." Three days later, the United States cut its entire $70 million dollar aid budget to Yemen. Phyllis Bennis, *Before and After: U.S. Foreign Policy and the September 11th Crisis* (Northampton, MA: Interlink, 2002).

22. Sarah Graham-Brown and Chris Toensing, *Why Another War? A Backgrounder on the Iraq Crisis* (Washington, DC: Middle East Research and Information Project, 2002); hereafter *MERIP*.

23. The following account of U.S. massacres during the 1991 war has been contributed by Jacob Levich.

24. On January 24, *only one week* after the air assault began, Gen. Colin Powell declared that the United States had achieved "air superiority"—typically defined as "that degree of dominance in the air that permits friendly land, sea, and air force to operate at a given time and place without prohibitive interference by opposing force"—and that Iraq's nuclear program had been destroyed. Dan Balz and Rick Atkinson, "Powell Vows to Isolate Iraqi Army and 'Kill It,'" *Washington Post*, 24 January 1991. Yet bombing raids continued for *an additional five weeks*. The intent can only have been punitive.

25. U.S. Air Force, "Airpower in the Gulf War," *Air and Space Power Mentoring Guide Essays II* (Maxwell Air Force Base, Ala.: Air University Press, 1999), pp. 72-73.

26. John MacArthur, *Second Front: Censorship and Propaganda in the Gulf War* (New York: Hill and Wang, 1993), p. 161.
27. "U.S. Urged to Ban Cluster Bombs," *Boston Globe*, 18 December 2002.
28. Human Rights Watch, *Needless Deaths in the Gulf War: Civilian Casualties During the Air Campaign and Violations of the Laws of War* (New York: Human Rights Watch, 1991).
29. MEDACT, *Collateral Damage: The Health and Environmental Costs of War on Iraq*, Report, November 2002. This conservative figure excludes the hundreds of thousands killed indirectly, though intentionally, by the strategic targeting of water plants and other civilian infrastructure. Reliable figures for death and damage may never be discovered, since both sides had reason to minimize their true extent.
30. Ibid. ; "Washington Whispers," *U.S. News & World Report*, 1 April 1991.
31. Patrick Sloyan, "Buried Alive," *Newsday*, 12 September 1991.
32. *Newsday* report quoted in Douglas Kellner, *The Persian Gulf TV War* (Boulder, Co.: Westview Press, 1992)
33. Quoted in William Boot, "What We Saw; What We Learned," *Columbia Journalism Review*, May/June 1991.
34. Testimony of Joyce Chediak before the Commission of Inquiry for the International War Crimes Tribunal, 11 May 1991, as quoted in *Time*, 18 March 1991.
35. S. Muralidharan, *Frontline*, 12 October 2001; Thomas J. Nagy, "The Secret Behind the Sanctions", *The Progressive*, September 2001.
36. *MERIP*, p. 6.
37. Anthony Arnove, "Iraq Under Siege: Ten Years On", *Monthly Review*, December 2000.
38. *MERIP*, p. 7.
39. Arnove, "Iraq Under Siege,"p. 17.
40. *MERIP*, p. 8.
41. *The Economist*, 8 April 2000, cited in Arnove, "Iraq Under Siege,"p. 23.
42. *Los Angeles Times*, 19 June 2002.
43. Reuters, 30 July 2002.
44. *MERIP*, p. 15.
45. Michael Theodoulou and Roland Watson, "West Sees Glittering Prizes Ahead in Giant Oilfields," *Times* (London), 11 July 2002.
46. Cited in "The Word from the CIA: It's the Oil, Stupid," *The Age*, 23 September 2002.
47. These two countries and China had already been favored by Baghdad in trade, garnering $5.48 billion of the $18.29 billion in contracts approved by the UN. *MERIP*, p. 9.
48. *Wall Street Journal*, 19 September 2002.
49. *Observer*, 6 October 2002.
50. Ibid.

51. Ibid.

52. Dan Morgan and David B. Ottoway, "In Iraqi War Scenario, Oil Is the Key Issue; U.S. Drillers Eye Huge Petroleum Pool," *Washington Post*, 15 September 2002.

53. Ibid.

54. *Observer*, 3 November 2002. If despite this the U.K. is onboard for the invasion, it is because they have identified their interests overall with the United States offensive. Moreover, it is unlikely that they would be shut out of Iraq altogether, merely that they would have to get behind the Americans in the queue.

55. Neil Mackay, *Sunday Herald*, 15 September 2002; emphasis added.

3. The Real Reasons for the Invasion of Iraq—And Beyond

1. Neil Mackay, "Bush Planned Iraq 'Regime Change' Before Becoming President," *Sunday Herald*, 15 September 2002.

2. John Pilger, *New Statesman*, 16 December 2002.

3. *Washington Post*, 6 August 2002.

4. The presentation ends on the following cryptic note:
   Grand strategy for the Middle East:
   —Iraq is the tactical pivot
   —Saudi Arabia the strategic pivot
   —Egypt the prize.
   Presumably the first two phrases mean that invading Iraq offers a point of entry for the capture of Saudi Arabia. However, the last phrase remains obscure.

5. "Iraq War Hawks Have Plans to Re-Shape Entire Mideast," *Boston Globe*, 10 September 2002. Here is a further sample of current thinking among American policy makers:

   > The anti-Saudi views expressed in the briefing appear especially popular among neo-conservative foreign policy thinkers, which is a relatively small but influential group within the Bush administration. "I think it is a mistake to consider Saudi Arabia a friendly country," said Kenneth Adelman, a former aide to defense secretary Donald H. Rumsfeld, who is a member of the Defense Policy Board but didn' t attend the July 10 meeting. He said the view that Saudi Arabia is an adversary of the United States "is certainly more prevalent view than it was a year ago."
   >
   > In recent weeks, two neo-conservative magazines have run articles similar in tone to the Pentagon briefing. The July 15 issue of the *Weekly Standard*, which is edited by William Kristol, a former chief of staff for [former vice president] Quayle [and chairman of the Project for the New American Century], predicted "The Coming Saudi Showdown." The current issue of *Commentary*, which is pub-

lished by the American Jewish Committee, contains an article titled, "Our Enemies, the Saudis."

"More and more people are making parts of this argument, and a few all of it," said Eliot Cohen, a Johns Hopkins University expert on military strategy. "Saudi Arabia used to have lots of apologists in this country.... Now there are very few, and most of those with substantial economic interests or long standing ties there." Cohen, a member of the Defense Policy Board, declined to discuss its deliberations. But he did say that he views Saudi Arabia more as a problem than an enemy. "The deal that they cut with fundamentalism is most definitely a threat, [so] I would say that Saudi Arabia is a huge problem for us," he said. But that view is far from dominant in the U.S. government, others said.

"The drums are beginning to beat on Saudi Arabia," said Robert Oakley, a former U.S. ambassador to Pakistan who consults frequently with the U.S. military. *Washington Post*, 6 June 2002.

Cohen's mention of "those with substantial economic interests" in Saudi Arabia probably refers to former U.S. secretary of state Henry Kissinger, whose consulting firm counts the House of Saud among its most important clients. He appears now to represent a minority in the American establishment.

6. "Saudis Withdraw Billions of Dollars from U.S.," *Financial Times*, 8 August 2002.

7. Mo Mowlam, "The Real Goal Is the Seizure of Saudi Oil," *The Guardian*, 5 September 2002; emphasis added.

8. "More to Iraq war than just Saddam? U.S. has wider strategic aims, says an international conference," *Business Times*, 25 September 2002; emphasis added.

9. "Sharon's Plan Is to Drive Palestinians Across the Jordan," *Daily Telegraph*, 28 April 2002.

10. Eric Margolis, "Bush's Mideast Plan: Conquer and Divide," *Toronto Sun*, 8 December 2002.

11. Officials in the administration are quoted by the *New York Times* (11 October 2002) as saying that Iraq would be placed under U.S. military rule for an extended spell. More recently, as the United States pressed for French, German, and Russian support for its planned invasion, U.S. officials were quoted as preferring "international rule"—i.e. the involvement of other countries as well in policing post-invasion Iraq. "U.S. Adopts Kosovo Model to Follow War," *Los Angeles Times-Washington Post* News Service, 9 December 2002.

12. In a (London) *Times* interview, Sharon has called for Iran to be attacked the moment the invasion of Iraq is complete; Stephen Farrell, Robert Thomson, and Danielle Haas, "Attack Iran the Day Iraq War Ends,

Demands Israel," *Times,* 5 November 2002.

13. Cited in David N. Gibbs, "Washington's New Interventionism: U.S. Hegemony and Inter-Imperialist Rivalries," *Monthly Review*, September 2001.

14. Nicholas Lemann, *The New Yorker,* 1 April 2002; emphasis added.

15. Even the spread of biotechnology—which the United States and its corporations, seeing the prospect of massive commercial gain, have been thrusting on the rest of the world—is introduced: "The United States should help bring these benefits [of biotechnology] to the 800 million people, including 300 million children, who still suffer from hunger and deprivation." In line with this, the United States and the UN's Food and Agricultural Organization have been pressing genetically modified (GM) grain as food aid on famine-struck African nations who, for fear of the havoc that could be wreaked in their agriculture, are refusing it. The latter's refusal has become the occasion for veiled threats by the United States that the GM grain will be reached to their populations by military intervention.

16. Richard Norton-Taylor, "The New Nukes," *Guardian*, 6 August 2002.

17. *Washington Post*, 10 June 2002.

18. Jonathan Steele, *The Guardian*, 20 August 2002.

19. *Counterpunch*, 8 May 2002.

20. William Arkin, *Los Angeles Times*, 27 October 2002; emphasis added.

21. *New York Times*, 19 February 2002.

22. FAIR Media Advisory, "The Office of Strategic Influence is gone, but are its programs in place?," 27 November 2002.

23. Cited in ibid., William Arkin, *Los Angeles Times*, 24 November 2002.

24. Bill Vann, "Ultimatum to Europe in advance of Iraq war—U.S. demands total impunity on war crimes," www.wsws.org, 12 October 2002.

25. William Neikirk, *Chicago Tribune*, 15B1 8 December 2002.

26. Robert Brenner, "Enron Metastasized: Scandals and the Economy," *Against the Current*, September-October 2002.

27. *Economist*, 10 May 1998.

28. Neikirk, *Chicago Tribune*, 15-18 December 2002.

29. Brenner, "Enron Metastasized: Scandals and the Economy."

30. *Economist*, 28 September 2002.

31. See Harry Magdoff and Paul Sweezy, *Stagnation and the Financial Explosion* (New York: Monthly Review Press, 1987), p. 83, Chart 2.

32. Japan is also the world's largest creditor and saver, the possessor of a giant trade surplus and has the world's largest foreign exchange reserves.

33. Magdoff and Sweezy, *Stagnation and the Financial Explosion*, p. 35.

34. Brenner, "Enron Metastasized: Scandals and the Economy."

35. *Economist*, 28 September 2002.

36. Ibid.

37. Arjun Makhijani, "Saddam's Last Laugh: The Dollar Could Be Headed for Hard Times If OPEC Switches to the Euro," www.TomPaine.com, 9 March 2001.

38. Radio Free Europe, "Iraq: Baghdad Moves to the Euro," 1 November 2000; "Iraq uses the euro in its trade deals," www.ArabicNews.com, 7 September 2001.
39. *Iran News,* 29 December 2001.
40. "Iran sees euro as way to 'free' itself from the United States dollar,"Agence France Presse, 31 December 2001.
41. "Protest by switching oil trade from dollar to euro," *Oil and Gas International,* 15 April 2002.
42. *Asia Times,* 19 May 2001.
43. Brenner, "Enron Metastasized: Scandals and the Economy."
44. Nick Beams, "Dollar crisis may be close at hand," www.wsws.org, 18 June 2002.
45. Christopher Swann, "Dollar slide could gather dangerous speed," *Financial Times,* 25 June 2002.
46. C. Fred Bergsten, "America's Two-Front Economic Conflict," *Foreign Affairs,* MarchBA pril 2001.
47. Ibid.
48. Jane Perlez, "China Races to Replace U.S. as Economic Power in Asia," *New York Times,* 27 June 2002.
49. Edward L. Morse and James Richard, "The Battle for Energy Dominance," *Foreign Affairs,* March-April 2002; emphasis added.
50. There are three reasons for the recent U.S.-engineered unsuccessful coup in Venezuela, and the current as yet unsuccessful repeat performance. First, under the leadership of Hugo Chavez, Venezuela is carrying out certain pro-people economic changes, extracting better terms from the oil multinationals, defying U.S. hegemony, and trying to help others who are similarly doing so—thus providing an example very dangerous for the U.S. grip over the rest of Latin America. Secondly, Venezuela is the biggest oil exporter in the Western hemisphere, and a major source of U.S. imports. Thirdly, Chavez has been taking certain initiatives to revive OPEC and free it of American influence. In August 2000, he invited American and British fury with a visit to Baghdad where he convinced Iraq of the need for maintaining OPEC production restraints to prevent a fall in oil prices. On the same trip he also visited Iran and Indonesia, attempting to weld unity among OPEC. Leon Barkho, "Venezuela's Chavez Holds Iraq Talks,"Associated Press, 11 August 2000. "What can I do if they [Americans] get upset?" Chavez said after crossing into Iraq from Iran. "We have dignity and Venezuela is a sovereign country"—precisely the reasons why the Americans got upset.
51. Michael Peel, "U.S. Takes Good Look at West African Oil," *Financial Times,* 25 July 2002.
52. U.S. Energy Information Administration, "Top Petroleum Net Importers, 2000," www.eia.doe.gov.
53. Willy Wo-Lap Lam, "China opposes U.S. presence in Central Asia," CNN,

22 April 2002.

54. "China Races to Replace U.S. as Economic Power in Asia," *New York Times*, 28 June 2002.

55. "China digs for Middle East oil, U.S. gets fired up," Reuters, 24 September 2002.

56. At any rate in the United States there is at present no threat of inflation (as in the rest of the developed world as well); rather, the threat is of deflation, i.e. falling prices, which deters investment.

57. See "The Profits and Pitfalls of War in Iraq," www.stratfor.com.

58. No doubt arms manufacturers would get an instant boost. In the first half of 2002 the earnings of Northrop Grumman, General Dynamics, and Lockheed Martin improved. Most American arms firms are now able to raise funds easily from the capital market, which anticipates a big boost to sales and profits by 2004. "U.S. defense sector cashes in on Bush's war on terrorism," *Financial Times*, 19 July 2002. Demand from this sector will mitigate the recessionary trends somewhat.

59. See James K. Galbraith, "The Unbearable Costs of Empire," *The American Prospect*, 18 November 2002.

60. See statistics compiled by *Defense and the National Interest* online magazine, www.d-n-i.net.

61. William D. Nordhaus, "Iraq: The Economic Consequences of War," *New York Review of Books*, 5 December 2002.

62. Citing James R. Blaker, *United States Overseas Basing* (New York: Praeger, 1990) in "U.S. Military Bases and Empire," *Monthly Review*, March 2002.

63. Sally Buzbee, "U.S. Expands Military Ties Worldwide," Associated Press, 15 January 2002.

64. Jim Lobe, "Alarm bells ring over U.S. overseas military spending,"*Asia Times,* 9 February 2002.

65. *Los Angeles Times,* 6 January 2002, quoted in "U.S. Military Bases and Empire," *Monthly Review*, March 2002.

66. *Time,* 18 November 2002.

67. David Rohde, "Anti-American Feeling Rises in Pakistan as U.S. Confronts Iraq," 22 December 2002.

68. Jack Fairweather, "U.S. covers up killings of its troops in Kuwait," *Daily Telegraph*, 22 December 2002.

4. REHABILITATING COLONIALISM

1. See Cooper, "The Post-Modern State," in *Reordering the World: The Long-Term Implications of September 11*, ed. Mark Leonard (London: Foreign Policy Center, 2002) (Cooper's chapter is reproduced in www.epuget.com); Wolf, "The Need for a New Imperialism," *Financial Times*, 9 October 2001; and Paul Johnson, "Colonialism and the War Against Piracy," *Wall Street Journal*, 10 October 2001. Boot, Brzezinski, Kaplan, Ikenberry, and Rosen

are quoted in John Bellamy Foster, "The Rediscovery of Imperialism," *Monthly Review*, November 2002; Foster in turn cites Philip S. Golub, "The Dynamics of World Disorder: Westward in the Course of Empire," *Le Monde Diplomatique*, English Internet edition September 2002. Krauthammer and Fairbanks are quoted in Emily Eakin, "It Takes an Empire, Say Several U.S. Thinkers," *New York Times*, 1 April 2002, which also quotes Boot and Kaplan.

2. Here is Blair doing the packaging at the Labor Party conference in October 2002: "I believe this is a fight for freedom not only in the narrow sense of personal liberty but in the broader sense of each individual having the economic and social freedom to develop their potential to the full.... The starving, the wretched, the dispossessed, the ignorant, those living in want and squalor from the deserts of Northern Africa to the slums of Gaza to the mountain ranges of Afghanistan: they too are our cause."

3. *Times of India,* 21 December 2001.

4. See Marc W. Herold, "The Massacre at Kakarak," *Frontline*, 16 August 2002.

5. *Independent*, 12 June 2002; emphasis added. Khalilzad, an Afghan-born U.S. citizen, was earlier, like Karzai, an employee of the Texas oil company UNOCAL. That company, in its drive to lay a natural gas pipeline from Turkmenistan through Afghanistan to Pakistan and perhaps India, had funded and backed until 1998 the Taliban's drive to conquer Afghanistan. Khalilzad is now the United States special envoy for West Asia and Southwest Asia. Evidently he was not an elected delegate to the *loya jirga*, but participated in the role of viceroy, as it were.

6. *Times of India,* 21 November 2002, based on Bob Woodward, *Bush at War* (New York: Simon & Schuster, 2002).

7. *Asian Age,* 16 October 2002.

8. *Times of India,* 6 December 2001.

9. *Times of India,* 21 December 2001.

10. *Asian Age,* 15 September 2002.

11. Seema Mustafa, *Asian Age,* 21 November 2002.

12. *Times of India,* 4 June 2002.

13. *Asian Age,* 31 October 2002.

14. "U.S. to Seek Mideast Reforms; Programs Aim to Foster Democracy, and Education,"*Washington Post*, 21 August 2002.

15. "Iraq War Hawks Have Plans to Reshape Entire Mideast," *Boston Globe*, 10 September 2002.

16. *New York Times,* 11 October 2002.

17. "The Unbearable Costs of Empire," *American Prospect*, 18 November 2002.

18. *Christian Science Monitor,* 9 October 2002.

INDEX